MOTIVATING
Defiant & Disruptive Students
TO LEARN

To Joy Bach
For the sacrificial hours you spent editing and being
a cheerleader and for your selfless commitment to this project.
Thank you.

MOTIVATING
Defiant & Disruptive Students
TO LEARN

Positive
Classroom
Management
Strategies

Rich Korb

CORWIN
A SAGE Company

CORWIN
A SAGE Company

FOR INFORMATION:

Corwin
A SAGE Company
2455 Teller Road
Thousand Oaks, California 91320
(800) 233-9936
Fax: (800) 417-2466
www.corwin.com

SAGE Ltd.
1 Oliver's Yard
55 City Road
London EC1Y 1SP
United Kingdom

SAGE India Pvt. Ltd.
B 1/I 1 Mohan Cooperative Industrial Area
Mathura Road, New Delhi 110 044
India

SAGE Asia-Pacific Pte. Ltd.
33 Pekin Street #02-01
Far East Square
Singapore 048763

Acquisitions Editor: Hudson Perigo
Associate Editor: Allison Scott
Editorial Assistant: Lisa Whitney
Production Editor: Cassandra Margaret Seibel
Copy Editor: Cate Huisman
Typesetter: C&M Digitals (P) Ltd.
Proofreader: Sandy Zilka
Indexer: Joan Shapiro
Cover Designer: Scott Van Atta
Permissions Editor: Adele Hutchinson

Copyright © 2012 by Corwin

This book was self-published by the author in 2010.

Printed in the United States of America.

Library of Congress Cataloging-in-Publication Data

Korb, Rich.

Motivating defiant and disruptive students to learn : positive classroom management strategies / Rich Korb.

p. cm.
Includes bibliographical references and index.

ISBN 978-1-4522-0578-6 (pbk.)

1. Classroom management. 2. Problem children—Education. 3. Problem children—Behavior modification. 4. Motivation in education. I. Title.

LB3013.K665 2012 371.102′4—dc23 2011039018

This book is printed on acid-free paper.

12 13 14 15 16 10 9 8 7 6 5 4 3 2 1

Contents

Preface

Moving from suburban Seattle to the logging communities of southwestern Washington introduced me to the realities of culture shock. How things were done in middle-class America did not always work in rural America. Classroom management was no exception.

On the opening day of elk season, my classroom was occupied by only female students. Frustrated, angry, and thinking the students were playing a prank, I asked the girls where the boys were. They acted like I was from another planet. I suppose in a way I was, as the students called me "City Boy." Apparently the school board had a policy that excused boys to go hunting on opening day. My position on school attendance is that school comes first, unless you physically cannot get out of bed. I quickly learned that to survive, I was the one who needed to conform to the standards established by the local school board. I also learned to be creative within the limits of state law, school board policy, and building administration.

As the first year grew into 34 years, I found methods for working with the most challenging and difficult students. During my second year, a youngster named Chuck was enrolled in the keyboarding class I was teaching. Chuck was defiant, disruptive, and disrespectful to anyone he thought did not respect him. Chuck and I sat down and came up with a plan for him to pass the class. We were fortunate to have two classrooms separated by a full set of windows and a door. Chuck would get one room to himself, while I taught in the other. We agreed that he would complete his daily assignment during the class period; that he could walk around when he needed to, look out the window, and join the class if he sat and worked; and that he would not leave the classroom without permission. Chuck never rejoined the class, but he was never defiant, disruptive, or disrespectful with me. He did all of his assignments and passed the class.

Throughout my career I have always found a way to get on the same page with challenging students. Gaining a student's trust is the first step toward successful interventions.

Outlined within these pages are precepts that I have catalogued over the past 34 years as a teacher, administrator, and national presenter. These strategies will work if approached with a willing mind and compassionate heart for each student. This methodology in classroom management can be applied immediately in your classroom or building.

Throughout our journey of the strategies listed within these pages, you will notice references to our team. As in any work it takes a team and they need to be recognized as such. Join us in our tour of working with difficult students.

Enjoy the journey on your road to successful student management, and may you become encouraged and reenergized to work with challenging students.

Acknowledgments

My personal thanks are given to the many friends, teachers, and thousands of students who have contributed directly or indirectly to the strategies, methods, precepts, and ideas incorporated within these pages.

To my good friend and excellent writer John Trumbo, for his encouragement and storytelling approach, which caused this project to come to life—thanks a ton.

To my son David, for his hours of layout, presentation preparation, and technical support—you are my hero.

This book would not have been possible without this fine group of dedicated individuals.

Publisher's Acknowledgments

Corwin would like to thank the following individuals for taking the time to provide their editorial insight:

Rachel Aherns
Sixth Grade Science Teacher
Westridge Elementary School
West Des Moines Community School District
West Des Moines, IA

Dr. Melissa Albright, NBCT
Fifth Grade Communication Arts Teacher
Wilson's Creek School
Springfield Public Schools
Battlefield, MO

Neil MacNeill
Principal
Ellenbrook Primary School
Ellenbrook, Western Australia

Michelle Strom, NBCT
Middle School Language Arts Teacher
Fort Riley Middle School
Fort Riley, KS

About the Author

 **Rich Korb** has 34 years of experience as a successful educator and consultant working with difficult and at-risk students. He has taught both general and special education at all levels and has served as director of education at a ranch for delinquent youth.

His experience in working with difficult and defiant students has led him to develop a wealth of practical ideas that teachers and administrators can put to use immediately. He knows what works and what doesn't work when dealing with disruptive and defiant students.

Rich is a sought-after presenter and the author of *Accelerating Achievement Through Purposeful Assessment* as well as the current work. He is also an adjunct faculty member for Seattle Pacific University and Brandman University, Chapman University Systems, where he teaches a course in how to work with defiant and disruptive students.

Introduction

This book was written for all the teachers who struggle with diffi-cult students. It offers a powerful program of strategies that can be used in the classroom tomorrow. Each strategy has been classroom tested and can provide the control teachers desire. Teachers imple-menting the processes outlined within these pages will be able to increasingly enjoy their passion for teaching. Every new teacher can benefit from this book.

How can this occur? Students are a lot like horses. Through many years of working around horses, I have met individuals known as horse whisperers. Through their gentle yet firm persuasion, difficult and dangerous horses become manageable and productive.

This collection of interventions, strategies, and methods is dedi-cated to all the educators I call the student whisperers. They are the true champions who have survived the most challenging situations students have thrown at them. They are the educators who have learned how to maintain their calm in the face of adverse situations. They are the ones who have managed to use a gentle yet firm approach when they wanted to scream, run, and cry.

To those who have figured out the balance between classroom management and academic excellence—you are the true student whisperers.

1

Introduction to Student Motivation

During an undergraduate class, my professor proposed that we should always ask the most important question of all: Why? He stated, "If we stopped asking why, we would cease to grow in our understanding of life." Seeking to understand the *why* of student behavior is where we will begin our journey to successful student management.

Several years ago I read an article about understanding youngsters that began to answer the question of why they behave the way they do. Two important aspects of the article have always stuck with me: (1) youngsters bring their personal lives into the learning environment and (2) youngsters will do their best to keep the leader from finding out who they are on the inside by creating false outward appearances. But there is a great deal more to understand as well.

> Definition of an unruly individual: Difficult or impossible to discipline, control, or rule; resistant to control, fails to submit to rule or control; rebels against authority; one obstinately bent on having his or her own way; willfully and often perversely departs from what is desired, expected, or required.

Do any of these descriptors sound familiar with respect to unwanted behavior in your classroom or school?

Why Do Youngsters Misbehave?

Understanding the *why* in student behavior is necessary in order to create a nurturing learning environment for each student. Developing empathy for the disruptive and defiant student will open the door for learning and smooth operation of the classroom. Figure 1.1 shows that underlying causes for misbehavior can stem from both immaturity and lack of moral bearings.

Figure 1.1 Immature or Defiant? That Is the Question

The Litmus Test (K–12)

Immature (Socially Delayed)	PERSONALIZED TOWARD OTHERS	Defiant (Morally Challenged)
✓ Talkative		✓ Insubordinate
✓ Fidgety		✓ Accusatory
✓ Distracted		✓ Challenging
✓ Possessive		✓ Sabotaging

In addition to those listed in Figure 1.1, other forms of defiance might include attention getting or gang affiliation. Causes, in addition to immaturity or moral challenge as shown in the figure, might include peer pressure, poor nutrition, lack of sleep, problems at home, or problems with friends, other teachers, coaches, or an after school job. The list is endless. Therefore, it is not the form or the reason that is the issue; the issue is how the teacher is going to react to the manifestation of disruptive behavior.

Figure 1.2 provides a different perspective on causes, indicating how the interplay of skills and ambition may affect student behavior.

Figure 1.2   What Else Might Be Causing Misbehavior?

Brain Development

Research suggests that the cerebral cortex is still developing during the adolescent years, possibly into the early twenties. The cerebral cortex is the reasoning part of the brain. (Strauch, 2004, p. 12)

It has been documented through numerous interviews with teens regarding career path, substance abuse, and so forth that most of the interviewees could not give clear definitive answers as to why they made the choices they did. This understanding also increases our ability to deal effectively with defiant behavior, knowing it may in part be a function of adolescent brain development.

Role Identification

Outlined below are the various levels of emotional identity students share with adults outside the family unit. This outline helps teachers identify why students might be responding in a certain way, knowing that their responses are reflected in the stage of their development. When the teacher knows what the child's emotional needs are, the teacher is prepared to respond in a way that stabilizes the relationship.

Age Level	Role Identification
5–9	Parent Figure
10–13	Parent/Authority Figure
14–19	Authority Figure
20+	Coequal

Basic Needs

Abraham Maslow defined basic human needs, and Figure 1.3 shows youngsters' adaptations to those needs. When physical and safety needs (at the bottom of the charts) are met in the classroom, students naturally migrate toward the higher levels.

Students who come from supporting homes will advance more rapidly toward the higher levels of self-actualization. These students

Figure 1.3   Basic Human Needs

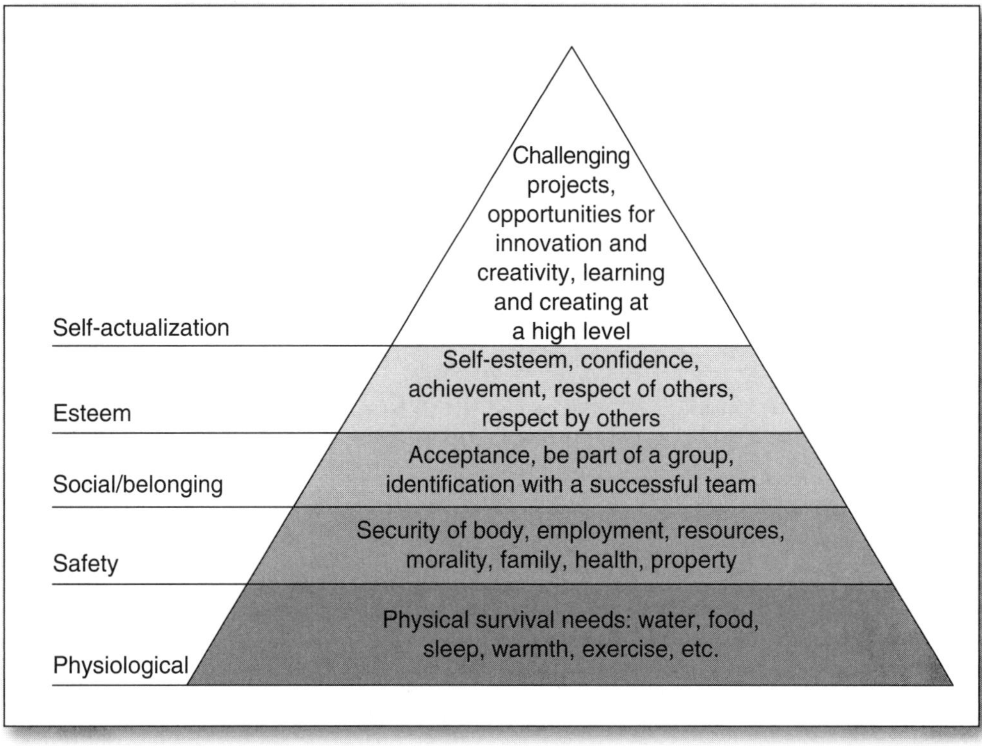

Source: Adapted from Maslow, 1943.

often find themselves at a relatively high level of safety and security, and they will not have a need to disrupt to gain the necessary attention. However, they can be more challenging if they feel their advancement toward self-esteem and recognition status is being hindered.

It is the students at the basic needs level who often become defiant and disruptive. Hence, they have a greater need for attention-getting antics. What they lack in home support is sought out in the classroom.

Motivation Defined

Once we understand the causes of negative behavior, we can move on to consider how to increase motivation toward appropriate behavior.

Definition Number 1: Something that leads or influences a person to do something.

We have all struggled with lethargic students who just won't get motivated. All we want is for them to do something—anything. The interventions outlined in this text will provide an impetus for the most reluctant learners to make an attempt at learning. The key is to get them to understand that any amount of effort will have a positive impact on their grades; in other words, effort will be valued over accuracy. They need to crawl first before they learn to walk and run.

Definition No. 2: Mental state, internal need, or outward goal that causes one to act.

Have you ever encountered an electronic device, only to discover you can't find the on switch? Working with hard-to-motivate students is much the same. The first stage in motivating disengaged students is to find out what causes them to get curious. Once we get them moving, the next challenge is to keep them moving until they are advancing on their own.

Motivation is usually defined by psychologists as the processes involved in arousing, directing and sustaining behaviour. (Ball, 1977, as quoted in Robb, 2001b, para. 2)

What the Research Says About Motivating Learners

From the literature on what motivates students to learn, the following key concepts were obtained from a wide collection of sources in a variety of formats. Here is a summary of what research has shown to be the top six motivators for learning (see also Figure 1.4):

1. Student control of learning. The focus here is learning. Assessment of learning styles and adapting lesson delivery is vital. If students feel they have their grades in their control (whether they actually do or not), the most resistant learners will engage and take ownership.

2. Relevance to student use and teacher's genuine interest. There is a dual emphasis between relevance and genuine interest. Why a lesson is important and how it connects to life is best embraced by the student when the teacher demonstrates genuine interest in the subject and students.

3. Teacher's enthusiasm. Teacher enthusiasm is vital. If a teacher has been assigned to a grade level or curriculum that he or she is not necessarily interested in, it's time to find the silver lining in the cloud. Students are perceptive and read their teachers' every action, reaction, and comment. Teachers must be excited about what they are bringing to the students if they expect the students to be interested.

4. Quick feedback and assignment return. Student performance is directly correlated to the time between assignment submission and return. Students' learning increases when they can make adjustments to errors in a timely fashion. Teachers should strive to return student work the next day.

Figure 1.4   The Motivational Web's Top Six Student Motivators for Learning

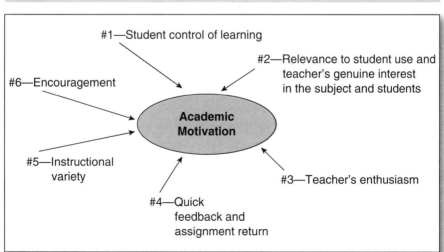

5. Instructional variety. Technology has provided the opportunity to deliver instruction in a variety of ways. Three shifts in approach to curriculum delivery during a 50- to 60-minute period will help student interest remain high and engaged. Shifting from lecture to group work to independent study keeps students connected and interested.

6. Encouragement. A simple pat on the back, a smiley face stamp, writing "Good Job!" or acknowledging effort can make a big difference in student performance.

In addition to the research findings listed above, our experience has shown that the following also help motivate students:

Relationships. When students trust a teacher's judgment and are truly appreciated for who they are, a working relationship begins to develop in which students are motivated to learn.

Rewards. In addition to verbal encouragement, a more tangible acknowledgment of effort or performance is always a stimulus for additional contributions.

Support. Teacher availability during instructional and noninstructional time is a motivator.

Honoring of personal values. Honoring home values (as long as they do not violate classroom values) provides motivation for students.

Creation of curiosity. Students are motivated when they are encouraged to explore and investigate new areas.

Clear expectations. Visible rules on assignment sheets, walls, and entry activities will keep the expectations consistently in front of the students.

Classroom climate. Classrooms should be inviting and safe, surrounded with charts and pictures that relate to the subject matter as well as points of interest contemporary to student life. Playing jazz (without words) during study time is also effective.

Firm, fair, purposeful action. When action needs to be taken, it should always have the purpose of motivating the student toward constructive ends, weaving the relationship.

De-emphasis on grades. Much has been written about the value of grades. Greater emphasis should be placed on effort and performance than grades when first attempting to move a student toward becoming a self-starter.

Organization. Students become more accountable when they see teachers being highly organized and maintaining a predictable learning environment.

Appropriate level of difficulty. Accommodations do not only apply to special needs students. Lesson designs aimed at challenging each student are necessary for a productive learning experience. High-performing students need additional opportunities for personal growth when the given task is completed. Methodical students should have the necessary time to complete the task without penalty.

Listening. It is important to listen and paraphrase what students are communicating in order for the teacher and student to move in the same direction.

What Happened to Natural Motivation?

With all this discussion of motivators that teachers can provide, readers might wonder what has become of intrinsic motivation. We were born self-starters, so what changed?

How we respond to experiences will drive us toward our full potential or divert our efforts away from what we can become. Many students come into the classroom with varying degrees and forms of support. Unmotivated students might come from an abusive situation or a home where social, moral, or religious values are misaligned with those of the school. Defiant and disruptive student behaviors are often driven by students' experiences in the home. Hence, they are no longer self-starters but are parroting the learning they have acquired outside themselves. Their choice to align with those outside behaviors needs to be redirected toward an understanding of personal choice. Defiant and disruptive students have chosen or been guided down the path they are on. It is the teacher's challenge to refocus the students toward becoming self-starters.

This is particularly hard at the elementary level due to the students' lack of life experiences. Elementary teachers need to take greater interest in and put more effort into younger students' motivation due to these students' psychological bonds with adults.

Adolescent students have more life experiences to reflect upon and need to be challenged regarding their future goals and dreams.

Our Experience With Motivating Youngsters

Our experience teaching youngsters has shown that the three F's in a youngster's life are

Friends

Fun

Food

Students will do anything to sit next to their friends. Allowing students to sit with their friends is a great motivator, and productive work can take place when they are allowed to work together. Threatening to separate friends is also a powerful motivator. It is amazing how cooperative students can become when they realize their relationship is about to be severed if a focus on learning is jeopardized for friendship.

When learning is perceived as fun, production increases, and students enjoy the process. Students become motivated when they buy into the learning process. Fun can be obtained through activity projects, variety in instructional methods, shifts in delivery approaches every 15 minutes, role-play, and educational games. Variety creates increased interest and a sense of anticipation.

Food is always a great motivator for youngsters of all ages. Taking away food from youngsters, especially teenagers, is a dangerous proposition. It's amazing what youngsters will do for food. Telling the class or disruptive students that they will be rewarded with food can create a situation where peer pressure will work in the teacher's favor. When all the students have something to gain, they will work together, and the disruptive students will likewise be motivated.

True Encounter

At the annual Cinco de Mayo assembly at our high school, the students had been patiently sitting in the bleachers for 30 minutes. As the assembly came to a close, a student representative stepped to the microphone announcing the fiesta to follow. She mentioned that a mariachi band, piñatas, and a taco truck were outside the gym. She also mentioned that one of the teachers was buying the first 20 tacos for the students who got there first. This announcement resulted in a stampede that the student leaders had a hard time stopping.

Connecting With Students

Connecting with students is essential to motivating them. There are three significant stages in connecting with students. They must occur one stage at a time, in the order shown here, if mutual learning and teaching are to take place.

First stage—connecting emotionally. Of the three relationship essentials, emotional bonding is by far the strongest in motivating the defiant and disruptive student. Students respond positively to acts of genuine kindness and sincerity, which often result in greater academic production. Gentle words of welcome and concern move the teacher-student relationship toward connection.

Second stage—understanding psychological barriers. Understanding the student's background, family, individualized education program (IEP), and interests is necessary to help motivate learning. Students are all independent agents who come with their own life experiences. Getting to the core of those experiences demonstrates care and compassion for the student. Once teachers understand why their students behave the way they do, they have a greater chance of aligning instructional theory and curriculum design for each student.

Third stage—modifying behavior. It will be necessary from time to time to redirect student behavior for the purpose of refocusing on classroom goals and objectives. Once the teacher and student have passed through the first two stages above, this process is made easier.

Differences in Values

Many teachers expect students to understand the classroom and school standards from the onset, which is a critical error. Moral expectations of the home and school can be vastly different. Teachers must be willing to accept that there can be a great difference between the two and be willing to address those differences in order to stimulate student motivation to learn.

There was a time in history when it was fairly safe to assume that most students came from homes with similar sets of values, values based on societal standards and traditions.

> **Remember This**
>
> Students do not necessarily come from the same value base as the teacher.

> **Remember This**
>
> The degree in behavior shifts will be different for each student, so each will feel a connection to the teacher at a different point in the learning process.

Today's society is composed of a myriad of different values, and this makes the management of youngsters a challenging endeavor. Predicting family support is difficult; therefore, it is necessary for the teacher to establish classroom expectations and be prepared to follow through with reinforcement of those expectations.

Modifying Student Behavior

What a student needs is an education. What a student wants is to take control of that education. As we have shown above, research makes a strong case that putting students in control of their learning is the best motivator. It's when a student attempts to take control of the *instruction* that problems begin. In situations like this, it's a good practice to keep your back to the wall and always face the class; if necessary, invite disruptive students to your desk.

Somewhere along life's journey, disruptive students have been taught that interrupting adults is the norm and adults are to acknowledge their requests whenever they make them. Thirty students all wanting the teacher's attention turns into chaos; therefore, students need parameters for their behavior and a process to obtain information they truly *need*. Students may need a lesson on identifying the difference between a need and a want. When personal needs are met, wants may be addressed.

Teach Students What Is Expected

All individuals are moral agents, and all have their own standards of right and wrong; for students, these typically are initially the standards they have learned at home. Once they are in school, however, classroom, school, and district rules serve as the moral compass by which each student must abide. It is the teacher's responsibility to enforce the code of conduct. Students who have been taught the code can be easily redirected to the acceptable path.

They, or someone else, might want the teacher to think they aren't able to follow school expectations. However, to make such an assumption is to set them up for failure. When the teacher constantly demands the right and challenges the wrong, students are easier to manage, and instructional time is increased.

Shift Directions to Retrieve Drifting Students

Students and teachers often approach the classroom with different expectations. Essentially, they are traveling parallel paths heading toward their educational goals. However, they are not always traveling at the same rate, and sometimes their paths diverge. Therefore, teachers must make efforts to connect with the students. When a student moves away from the educational goals of the curriculum and the teacher's direction, it becomes paramount for the teacher to shift direction in an attempt to come alongside the drifting student. As the teacher continues to make these adjustments to the student's behavior, the chances for personal connection and academic motivation improve. One degree in a shift of two parallel paths will ultimately lead to a connection.

> ### Remember This
>
> Mixing intervention strategies keeps defiant students off balance. They know that defiant behavior will be addressed; they just don't know when and what form it will take.

Teachers Cannot Save Every Child

This is one of the toughest admissions a teacher has to make; however, knowing you cannot save every child is a liberating realization. Some students are naturally defiant and disruptive by choice or influence. Working through this reality is hardest for young teachers who want to and believe they can save every child. This is simply not the case. Countless hours have been spent trying to reach the callused child, hours that could have been better spent assisting those who show signs of progress. Only through experience will a teacher realize when it is time to divert attention toward the students who are willing and able to learn.

Conclusion

Youngsters go through the natural process of physical, mental, emotional, and spiritual maturation. Accepting that youngsters are moral agents allows us to understand they are naturally going to challenge authority. Understanding that they often inherit this problem allows us to not take the behavior personally. In other words, you didn't raise the student, so don't own what you cannot control. When adolescents explode with defiance, what they are really looking for is the caring individual who will let them vent and then offer support in place of criticism. Students should be understood and accepted for who they are, not who they want people to think they are through dress, hair, tattoos, piercings, and disruptive behaviors.

True Encounter

The student had a vile mouth and did not care what anyone thought of him. When one of his teachers ignored his behavior, it provided him the opportunity to reflect on his comments. As this teacher stuck to the task of teaching and calling the student's bluff from time to time, the student became productive, a leader in this teacher's class, and a whistle-blower when other students were defiant. But in other classes, he continued to be defiant and showed little academic progress.

What was the difference? Was it the subject matter? Was it the seat assignment? The answer is yes, to a limited degree, in both of these areas. But more important, in the class where the student began to make a turnaround, he was allowed to push the teacher's buttons and get no direct response from the teacher. In the class where he was improving, he discovered the classroom and teacher were safe, and he did not need to put up defenses, because nobody was going to take up his challenge.

The turning point came when the student looked straight into the eyes of the teacher with the most defiant look he could muster and said, "F— you," in a soft and intimidating tone. The teacher's quiet response was, "Tell me something I haven't heard before." The student did not respond. He only looked confused, and he never acted out again.

After that, when the student was having a bad day, he would tell the teacher. More important, sometimes he would ask for a different seat, so he would not be tempted to act out. The student knew he was not going to be condemned, made an example of, or sent to the office, and that his parents would not be called. He felt understood and accepted for who he was, not what he wanted people to think he was.

This book will explore the reasons for disruptive and defiant behaviors and what can be done about them in the classroom. We will look at our responses to these behaviors and how we might be contributing to some of the problems. We will consider what motivates students and how to connect with them, as well as how to manage their behavior, both on an individual basis and from the standpoint of managing a whole classroom.

Enjoy the journey. There is hope for a brighter tomorrow. I'm confident you will find solutions within these pages that will help make your classroom a place you as well as your students look forward to being in each day.

Process and Apply

1. List defiant or disruptive behaviors you are experiencing in your classroom.

2. How could you use the defiant or disruptive behaviors as a means to develop a self-starter?

3. Define an unruly individual, and provide three detailed examples of unruly behavior from among the students you work with.

4. Define motivation, and share your understanding of what motivates youngsters.

5. Provide an example of parallel paths leading toward learning. What gets in the way of parallel paths intersecting?

6. Explain why emotional connectedness is essential at the onset of relationship building.

7. What role does the school play in developing constructive social values?

8. List the top six academic motivators and provide an explanation as to why they would be listed in the order they are given in this chapter.

9. Explain how the three F's could be useful in motivating youngsters.

10. How could having empathy for defiant and disruptive students create a more productive learning environment?

11. Why do youngsters misbehave?

12. Outline three reasons why physical and emotional development could be the cause for defiant and disruptive behavior.

13. What do we know from the stages of role identification that will help in developing self-starters?

14. Explain the difference between basic human needs and basic youngster needs.

2

Setting Up a Class Environment for Success

> We were in summer school. We sat in a portable classroom, and the temperature outside was 100 degrees. I stood in front of the group of eighth grade math students who needed to pass this class in order to get into high school. As I scanned the group, I sensed many had ended up in this class because they had been defiant, disruptive, noncompliant, disrespectful, and/or truant the year before. I had something they wanted, and they knew it.
>
> I decided I had two choices: (1) move forward with the instruction, or (2) start building relationships. I also knew that at some point I was going to give them unwelcome news resulting from poor performance, poor attendance, or low test scores. Experience told me most of these youngsters were bright. What they lacked was motivation. The way to get them motivated was to get to know them personally and begin to establish a common understanding of why they needed to learn math.

In this part of the journey to successful student management, we will explore the need to establish firm expectations and fair consequences. We will also develop strategies for the purpose of engaging challenging students from before the opening bell to when the final bell rings. The way you set up the class at the onset of the school year will greatly diminish power struggles. Referring to the classroom as a monarchy where the teacher is king or queen sends an important message to the students about roles. This way, students definitely know who is in charge.

It also opens the door to a brief history lesson on the Middle Ages, but be warned the knowledgeable students will bring up the Magna Carta and want to challenge the teacher's authority. Open discussions about who is in charge of the classroom should be encouraged, but only outside the classroom setting. Students will have a different perspective from yours on how things are going in the classroom.

Preparing Yourself for the School Year

Your Instructional Style

It is vital for teachers to know their instructional style prior to the arrival of students. This allows them to preplan how they will address unruly behavior and other challenging situations. The following style assessment is helpful in the process of preplanning.

Instructional styles, like management styles, can be generally described as falling into four categories: authoritarian, laissez-faire, indifferent, and authoritative. Individuals in leadership roles demonstrate each of these styles to varying degrees. Understanding your preferred style will greatly increase successful responses to student behavior.

When student learning style and teacher instructional style begin to align, greater production and higher motivation to learn occur. You might need to adjust your delivery style to align with your students' styles to ensure clarity. Hence, taking a survey of learning styles (see pp. 24–27) will provide the opportunity to meet students' needs. Don't sabotage the lesson by going with what is most comfortable for you. Explore ways to blend instructional style with learning styles, and eventually your students' learning styles and your instructional style begin to align.

Authoritarian

The authoritarian places firm limits and controls on the students. Students will often have assigned seats for the entire term. The desks are usually in straight rows. Students must be in their seats at the beginning of the class, and they frequently remain there throughout the period. This teacher rarely gives hall passes or recognizes excused absences.

Often it is quiet in this classroom. Students know they should not interrupt the teacher. Since verbal exchanges and discussion are discouraged, the authoritarian's students do not have the opportunity to learn or practice verbal communication skills.

This teacher prefers vigorous discipline and expects swift obedience. Failure to obey usually results in detention or a trip to the principal's office. In this classroom, students need to follow directions and not ask why.

Laissez-Faire

The laissez-faire teacher places few demands or controls on the students. The phrase "do your own thing" would describe this classroom. This teacher accepts the student's impulses and actions and is less likely to monitor behavior.

Indifferent

The indifferent teacher is not very involved in the classroom. This teacher places few demands, if any, on the students and appears generally uninterested. The indifferent teacher does not want to impose on the students. For this reason, the teacher often feels that lesson preparation is not worth the effort. Things like field trips and special projects are out of the question. Sometimes the teacher will use the same materials year after year.

Classroom discipline is lacking. This teacher may lack the skills, confidence, or courage to discipline.

The students sense and reflect the teacher's indifferent attitude. Accordingly, very little learning occurs. Everyone is just going through the motions. In this environment, the students have few opportunities to observe or practice communication skills. With few demands placed on them and little discipline, students have low motivation and lack self-control.

Authoritative

The authoritative teacher places limits and controls on the students but simultaneously encourages independence. This teacher often explains the reasons behind the rules and decisions. If a student is disruptive, the teacher offers a polite, but firm, reprimand. This teacher sometimes metes out discipline but only after careful consideration of the circumstances. The authoritative teacher is also open to considerable verbal interaction, including critical debates. The students know they may interrupt the teacher if they have a relevant question or comment. This environment offers the students the opportunity to learn and practice communication skills.

Your Curriculum and Subject Matter

Gaining a firm understanding of the curriculum allows the teacher to design varying methods of delivery. Curriculum serves as the foundation for instruction. With a solid foundation, the teacher can begin to manipulate the curriculum and tailor it to match their instructional style and student learning preference.

Throughout the course of a career, teachers are often assigned to teach subject matter of which they are not fully knowledgeable. But having a command of the subject is important. A dedication to serving the students with the best lessons backed by solid facts is essential. Students know when a teacher is struggling and will take advantage. Therefore, it is prudent for teachers to be honest when they don't know all the facts. It is even better if the teacher makes it a practice to get answers to students' questions as quickly as possible. Integrity plays a big role in student/teacher rapport.

When a teacher is excited about the subject, student level of interest also increases. Keeping student interest high is useful in maintaining a learning atmosphere. There is no substitute for enthusiasm.

Other Preparations for the School Year

In addition to identifying their instructional style and understanding the curriculum, there are several other things teachers can do before the school year begins that will help them be prepared to address challenging student behavior. Many of these are listed in this section.

The Classroom

The classroom should reflect the subject being presented. History classes should have décor related to history, and math classes should have décor related to math. Charts and posters promoting the subject assist in the motivation process. Objects of interest related to the subject give additional support to the learning. Additional school-related adornments (e.g., pictures of the school mascot, large printouts of school slogans) bring about a sense of ownership and oneness between teacher and students.

Establishing the learning space sets the tone for the classroom. Placing teachers' and paraprofessionals' stations in diagonally opposite corners provides for good viewing, listening, and assisting. A teacher's station at the back of the class tends to encourage a higher quality of production.

Meeting Needs of Specific Students

Sometimes a student needs to be set apart from the class to refocus on learning. A separate seat outside the main learning environment provides the necessary refocusing. Sometimes this seat becomes a permanent seat if the student is unable or unwilling to function responsibly in the class setting.

Too many students are not getting the sleep their developing bodies need. Students who are having trouble staying awake lack enough oxygen to their brain. To increase the blood flow, the student needs to stand and move around. It's a good idea to establish an area out of the direct viewing of the class where students can stand and not lean against something or bother other students. Students should be encouraged to take the initiative on their own without penalty.

Mobiles suspended from the ceiling assist students with attention concerns, such as attention deficit disorder (ADD)—the motion tends to create a subliminal form of relaxation.

Instructional Materials

Classroom materials are the manipulatives that drive instruction. Innovative teachers are usually well respected and have great success with all students, because they continue to look for ways to reach each of their students. (Failure to reach each student is not an option for these teachers.) Such teachers take an innovative approach to making good use of classroom materials to make learning enjoyable and challenging. The proper use of instructional materials can serve as motivational tools for the reluctant learner. Teacher-designed manipulatives cause a natural curiosity in students.

Worksheets

Preparation of worksheets is essential for keeping the lesson moving forward. Not having enough worksheets or the wrong ones will serve as a deterrent to the lesson and open the door for the defiant and disruptive student to capitalize on the disorganization.

Journals

A well-known method for assessing how interventions are working is through journal writing, so having a journal ready for each student is a good idea on Day 1. Entry activities (see Chapter 4) that build on past lessons are a great way to evaluate the student's growth and discover areas that need to be shored up. Daily journal writing is a good way to collect data on student ability.

Paperwork

Another necessary detail to the preparation of a successful start for the school year is the forms needed to be signed by parents. Much vital information needs to be shared between home and school to avoid conflicts between parent and teacher. It is essential to track forms accurately and account for all forms as the school year begins.

Information collected should include the following:

- **Parent/guardian contact information.** Although most school record systems provide parent and/or guardian contact information, students often know how to contact their parents better than the school does. It is helpful in cases of highly defiant and disruptive classes to have each student add this information (student and parent/guardian e-mail and home addresses, and work and cell phone numbers) to the Student Learning Survey (see pp. 24–27).
- **Probation officer contact information.** This tool is highly effective with students who have a probation officer assigned to them. Knowing that the teacher has access to the officer's e-mail and cell number is usually all it takes to keep court-supervised students motivated and productive.
- **Permission slips** for video viewing, field trips, and using the Internet.

Classroom Procedures

Teachers should have their standard procedures set and a plan to present them to students before the first day of school. These should include the following:

- **Order of the day plan.** Clearly written or projected goals and objectives for each day's lessons greatly reduce confusion and frustration for students and teacher. The entry activity and daily plan are useful in keeping students on track and the lesson moving forward.

- **Time schedule.** Related to the plan, posting a time schedule and a clock behind the teacher's desk helps keep the lesson moving forward and reduces the chances of disruption about class ending time. During instructional time, student focus should be on the lesson. Defiant and disruptive students often plan their disruptive behaviors based on time. Their tolerance level for managed time is strained when they need to stay focused for extended periods of time. When difficult students have to turn toward the teacher's desk to check the schedule and time, it serves as an alert for the teacher that there could be a disruption coming. This strategy serves as a type of seismograph that warns when the ground is beginning to shake. (When disruptive and defiant students look to see what the teacher is doing during study time, this also serves as a warning sign of impending disruption.) Posting the time schedules behind the teacher's station creates an atmosphere focused on learning and not the time. Students don't like to turn toward the teacher to check the time.

- **Evacuation routes.** Student knowledge of evacuation routes and emergency procedures is critical in times of crisis. Visible and updated procedures are necessary and should be reviewed regularly. A copy of such procedures should accompany lesson plans left for substitute teachers.

- **Office referral procedures.** Usually, school administrators provide direction about when and how office referrals are to be used. The teacher needs to have a clear understanding about how the referral system works from the time the referral is submitted to the time action is taken by the administration. Support from the office is highly dependent upon the proper use of the referral process.

- **Attendance polices.** Students should receive specific definitions of excused absences, unexcused absences, and tardies, including the maximum number of absences that will be allowed before a student is denied credit for the class.

- **Other standard procedures.** The section in Chapter 4 (p. 81) on Dealing With Interruptions includes some other procedures that should be established with administration and introduced to students at the beginning of the school year.

The First Day of Class

The structure of the first day of class might look like this:

1. Meet the students at the door with a genuine greeting, and provide each with a 3 × 5 card. Personalized contact for each student might be a handshake or a word of welcome. Then welcome the whole class with a sincere comment of appreciation for their being there.

2. Take attendance using the procedure on pages 27–28.

3. Direct students to fill out the 3 × 5 cards using the procedure for preassessment listed on page 24.

4. Ask students to fill out a Student Interest Survey, shown on page 24.

5. Set your standards: With the whole class, review class expectations and consequences for unacceptable behavior.

6. At the end of class, thank the students for their participation and input. Dismiss them with a genuine parting comment, such as "Have a good day," "Don't do anything I wouldn't do," or "See you tomorrow."

Assessing Student Interests and Abilities

At the onset of the school year (recommended on the first day of class) it is important to do a little fact finding. It is always useful at the beginning of the new term (or when new students enter your class) to determine students' strengths and weaknesses. For this purpose, you can use the Student Interest Survey. This assessment tool is helpful in evaluating students' personal interests as well as the level of comprehension and skills they have. This information will help guide instruction as well as provide useful information about student retention and knowledge base.

Gaining as much information as possible about each student will lead toward a bonding between student and teacher. The bond will become essential in the instructional and learning process throughout the year. Emotional and psychological connections with students are the two primary aspects in establishing a relationship. Understanding the driving forces in a student's life will provide you with powerful information to address student behavior.

The Student Interest Survey provides valuable information a teacher can use to gain an understanding of student interests and future plans. When combined with results from the Student Learning Survey, the information can be used to design lessons aimed at student interests while shoring up weak areas. Understanding student learning styles is useful in motivating students. A knowledge of student interests combined with an understanding of how each student learns will enable you to create a rich environment for student and teacher growth. Based on the learning styles represented in your class, you can adjust percentages of instructional style and time to align with their style preferences.

Student Interest Survey

You can print out cards specifically for this purpose, or just write this list of requested information on the board and ask students to write the answers on blank 3 × 5 cards.

---

3 × 5 Student Interest Survey

Name:

Date:

Period:

Class Title:

1. If you had all the money and time you wanted, what would you do?
2. Do you want just to pass this class, or is the grade important?
3. What do you want to learn in this class?
4. How do you learn best? (Circle the approach or approaches below that apply to you.)

   Figuring things out (kinesthetic)

   Being told how to do something (auditory)

   Watching (visual)

Student Learning Survey

The table below shows the responses to an interest survey we have used with our classes. It shows the combined responses of our students—those in the left column indicate the percentage of regular education students who chose this response, and those in the right column show the percentage of special education students who chose this response. (A total of 142 regular education students and 88 special education students provided responses for the percentages shown here.) Readers can remove the percentages and insert checkboxes to create blank survey sheets for use in their own classrooms.

	Regular Education Students	Special Education Students
I learn best by . . .		
a. being shown how to do something.	66%	56%
b. listening to someone explain.	17%	31%
c. figuring it out by myself.	17%	13%
I study best when . . .		
a. I can listen to my music.	67%	62%
b. music or TV is playing.	6%	24%
c. it is quiet.	27%	14%
Watching a movie really helps me learn new information.		
Yes	100%	70%
No	0%	30%
Computers help me with my writing.		
Yes	71%	78%
No	29%	22%
Computers help me with my reading.		
Yes	45%	50%
No	55%	50%

(Continued)

(Continued)

	Regular Education Students	Special Education Students
Computers help me with my math.		
Yes	40%	59%
No	60%	41%
What other approaches help you learn?		
	1. Projects	1. Going through a process step by step
	2. Lectures	2. Working with a partner
	3. Working with a group	3. Working alone
	4. Reading	4. Being reminded to stay on focus
	5. Taking notes	
	6. Worksheets	
	7. Working independently	
	8. Using a calculator	
Note: These activities are listed in order of student preference; that is, the higher an activity appears on a list, the greater the number of students who preferred it.		
The best way to treat me when I make a mistake on schoolwork is to . . .		
a. talk with me in private.	38%	NA
b. tell me right then.	31%	NA
c. write me a note.	31%	NA
The best way to treat me when I make a mistake with school rules is to . . .		
a. talk with me in private.	59%	NA

	Regular Education Students	Special Education Students
b. tell me right then.	24%	NA
c. write me a note.	17%	NA
I should be allowed to redo assignments . . .		
a. twice.	43%	NA
b. until I'm happy with my score.	43%	NA
c. three times.	14%	NA
The best reward when I do well in school is . . .		
a. coupons for fast food restaurants.	46%	48%
b. hearing that I did a good job.	35%	31%
c. getting tickets I can collect and trade for prizes.	19%	21%
I should be graded on my . . .		
a. effort.	60%	66%
b. scores.	25%	20%
c. attendance.	15%	14%

Taking Attendance

The process of taking attendance should be personalized and student driven. For example, students might be asked to say their own first names after you call out their last names from the roll list.

The following process works magic when taking attendance for the first time with students you have never met:

1. Review names before the class gathers.

2. Offer an upfront disclaimer to indicate you realize you will be mispronouncing some names the first time.

3. Call each student's last name, and have the student give his or her first name.

4. Apologize for any mispronunciations, and ask students for the name they would like you to use with them.

5. Repeat each name to make sure you know how to pronounce it correctly.

Another good approach is to visit all students at their desks, and ask them to show you their names on your list. Use their names often for reinforcement and relationship building.

Expectations and Consequences

To give instruction its best chance for success, it is important to establish expectations and consequences during the first few days of the class. At the beginning of the school year or term, when classroom expectations and consequences are taught, students gain an understanding of what is expected and the consequences that will follow unacceptable behavior. During the first class meeting, clear expectations of when to discuss personal issues must be explained. Defiant and disruptive students will try to derail the teacher's attempts to engage the class in learning if these expectations are not firmly established and reviewed each time a disruption surfaces.

This must be followed by consistent enforcement on a daily basis until the expectations become a natural function of the classroom. Occasional review of classroom expectations and consequences following long periods of separation (Thanksgiving, Christmas, Spring Break) will be necessary, as home and school expectations are often different. Students will voluntarily or involuntarily forget the school house rules.

If consequences have been enforced on a consistent basis throughout the school year, students will understand that their behavior will not be tolerated very long. The students know it is only a matter of time until the teacher will confront defiant behavior.

Tightly structured classrooms provide control and parameters for the whole class, especially the defiant and disruptive students. After developing the class standards, ask yourself how students can twist your efforts, and then plan how you will deal with this behavior. One approach is to accept student input and seek to qualify potentially disruptive comments through paraphrasing. Seeking to understand will keep defiant and disruptive students in check while they try to disrupt the process. It is hard work to turn the negatives into positives, yet it is necessary to keep the instruction moving forward.

One more thing to do on Day 1 is to set a precedent by using an entry activity as described in Chapter 4. The Preassessment Cards can serve as this activity on your first day.

The Second Day of Class

As strong as expectations and consequences might be, consistency in follow-through is equally important. Assessing students' understanding from the previous day, and documenting their understanding, is useful when expectations need to be enforced.

Class Operation Test

This test is designed to strengthen students' understanding of class expectations and consequences while establishing the moral standards for the classroom. It can also be very effective for reinforcing and teaching school expectations as provided in student handbooks. No more than ten items should on the assessment. Fewer items tighten the parameters for students to operate within and reduce the avenues for challenges by disruptive students.

The test requires a score of 100%; this helps ensure that students understand class expectations and consequences. Students should be required to retake the test until a perfect score is obtained.

Documentation is important for student accountability, so written records of this test and student scores should be maintained. Reinforcement of class standards becomes easier with documentation when a student needs intervention.

The sample class operation test shown below includes just five questions that we have used to help students learn expectations and consequences for our classes. (Terms such as "the four P's" and "CBIP" are explained in Chapters 3 and 4.)

Class Operation Test

Directions—Circle the letter that answers the question correctly.

1. Where am I supposed to be when the tardy bell rings?
   a. in the room
   b. at my desk and working
   c. hanging around the classroom door

2. When I come to class, I am expected to . . .
   a. Visit with my friends.
   b. Ask the teacher what we are doing today.
   c. Get my folder, go to my desk, and start on the assignment on the screen.

(Continued)

(Continued)

3. What are the four P's?

   a. play, pals, party, plagiarism
   b. punctual, prepared, productive, polite
   c. politics, party, passing time, planets

4. Which of the following has the biggest impact on my grade?

   a. the performance sheet
   b. my assignments
   c. test scores

5. Consequences for violation of the above expectations can result in . . .

   a. lunch detention, CBIP, and removal from class
   b. being sent to the office
   c. parent phone call

Process and Apply

1. Explain your classroom instructional style and how your style will advance the learning of all your students.

2. How is the awareness of correct student name pronunciation necessary in managing disruptive student behavior?

3. How could the preassessment of student interests help in building relationships with difficult students?

4. Design a 3×5 card entry activity that fits your grade level. Be sure to include pertinent information germane to your needs. This activity must have a focus on how you will assess learning styles.

5. Explain how you could use figures (percentages) from the Student Learning Survey results to guide your planning for lessons and managing student behavior.

6. Outline your first day of class.

7. Provide three reasons the class operation test would be beneficial in working with defiant and disruptive students.

3

Behavior Improvement Strategies for Individual Students

Aaron would not stop talking and disrupting the class. It seemed he always had something more important to share than the lesson content. No amount of discussion or persuasion was working. The harder I tried to connect with him, the more I realized he was just not interested in the lessons. He wanted to pass the class with minimal effort and preferred I stay out of his way.

Aaron knew his behavior did not align with classroom expectations. However, his personal needs far surpassed his desire to cooperate with classroom rules. Knowing that confession of wrong is always a good beginning point in mending a relationship, we began there. Aaron knew all the answers about proper behavior. Aaron could articulate what he needed to do. He just would not bring himself to follow through with what needed to be done to survive in the classroom setting.

What gave Aaron and me a chance for success was the entry activity mentioned in the previous chapter and described at length in Chapter 4. He had a starting point each day and knew that passing the class was predicated upon his completing the entry activity within five minutes after the tardy bell. The challenge was keeping the academic motivation high and disruptions low once the entry activity ended.

The strategies in this chapter provide hope and encouragement when facing tough situations in our journey to successful student management.

Defining Acceptable Behavior

Remember This
Moral development of the student is the focus. Moral change is where true behavior modification begins. The student who is required to look into the proverbial mirror of their own actions will start to align with class expectations. When the students are in control of their own destiny, perceived or real, positive growth can begin.

Acceptable behavior takes place when the student produces what is expected. Most students, when walked through a process of behavior correction, don't need to pass through it again. If their dignity has been preserved, they become willing to follow class expectations in the future. There have been times when some of these students become student coaches for other unruly classmates. Overall, the students begin to control themselves.

When clear expectations and consequences are presented, students are forced into a moral decision. They are going to accept or resist the expected behavior. Either way, the student's choice must be acknowledged with positive or negative consequences. Affirmation of the choice is central to defining desired behavior.

This is the hardest part of teaching. Most teachers did not go into teaching to work on student behavior. However, difficult behavior is a given in any population.

Cognitive Processing

To help students improve their behavior, understanding what is taking place in their thoughts can be very helpful. The drawing in Figure 3.1 from Bandler and Grinder (1979) provides general assistance. At any given time, students are processing visual and auditory input as well as internal dialogue or feelings. Attention to a student's thought process is useful. Is the student responding to visual or auditory clues, or is the student processing? Understanding what is going on internally with the student enables the teacher to avoid added interactive inquiry, such as additional questioning or paraphrasing, which could escalate the student's anxiety. Body language and eye response will provide necessary information the teacher will need to further assist the student.

Additionally, being aware of cultural behaviors is vital in understanding what is going on with your students. Each culture group has learned or traditional mannerisms that serve as clues. A quick study of the culture groups you serve will enhance their learning process and help you determine which behaviors are cultural and which are purely defiant and disruptive by student choice.

What we have discovered when working with defiant and disruptive students is that generally (based on culture), there is an avoidance of eye contact. When being questioned about disruptive behavior, the student will usually look toward the floor. Eye movement is generally to the right.

This can be helpful, but is not to be considered the rule. It is important to keep societal expectations in mind when considering these cues. In some cultures, looking down is expected; in others, youngsters are expected to look their elders in the eye. Teachers should bear such differences in mind when considering how they define acceptable behavior.

Figure 3.1   Cognitive Processing (K–12)

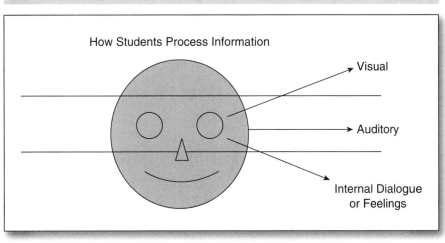

Source: Adapted from Bandler and Grinder, 1979, as seen in Payne, 2005, pp. 97–100.

The Daily Performance Sheet

The document shown on page 34—the Daily Performance Sheet, or DPS—is helpful in achieving acceptable behavior for a variety of reasons. Teachers find this recording device quick and helpful for holding students accountable and focused. Accountability is the main benefit.

The DPS lists what we call the four P's of accountability. When Fortune 500 corporate executives were asked what desirable traits they looked for in their employees, these are what they listed as the top four—punctual, prepared, productive, and polite. Teachers are preparing students for the workforce, and these skills in self-management are as necessary as academic skills. As educators work toward developing the minds and attitudes of youngsters, it is vital to keep these four P's in mind. These then become the expectations for the students.

The following are the definitions of the four P's:

Punctual: The student is in her seat and working on the entry activity when the tardy bell rings.

Prepared: The student has all required materials at her seat before the tardy bell rings.

Productive: The student completes all requirements for the lesson.

Polite: The student demonstrates appropriate classroom behavior and avoids disrupting the class through inappropriate language or behavior as outlined by the teacher.

Daily Performance Sheet

Note: The corporate workplace requires employees to be

Punctual: Working when tardy bell rings

Prepared: Have all required materials when tardy bell rings

Productive: Daily assignment(s) completed at end of period

Polite: Appropriate language and behavior

Name: _____

Period: _____

	Punctual	Prepared	Productive	Entry Quiz	Polite	Week Ending
						Date: _____
M	0 1	0 1	012345	0123	0 1	
TU	0 1	0 1	012345	0123	0 1	
WE	0 1	0 1	012345	0123	0 1	
TH	0 1	0 1	012345	0123	0 1	
F	0 1	0 1	012345	0123	0 1	Week Total: ___

Using the DPS

The sheet is used to score each student's overall performance on these five parameters every day. If, for example, a student completes the daily entry activity/quiz (see Chapter 4) and other assignments on Tuesday, that student would receive a high rating, and the number 4 should be circled on the Productive scale for Tuesday. If the student does not complete assignments, the score would be low (0 to 2), depending on how many of the assignments were completed. At the end of the week, students add up the circled numbers to compute the week's total. This allows students to keep track of their grades on a daily basis; they don't need to wait for the teacher to post grades. Instant feedback creates a higher level of accountability and gives students an opportunity to alter behaviors that are having a negative impact on their grades.

Marking scores on the DPS can be done in a variety of ways. Younger students and special needs students benefit by having the teacher assist them in assigning themselves scores at the end of each academic session. Older students can score themselves.

Collection of the DPS can be done at the end of the period, day, or week. In special cases, the DPS can be used on an individual basis as well.

To increase the validity of the DPS, it is necessary to verify the student's scores. Adjusting the score to reflect the teacher's perspective on the student's performance is very important. The feedback to the student is necessary for providing support and validity. Changing a score upward tells the student your judgment of their behavior is more favorable than theirs. Changing a score downward informs the student that your expectations are not being met. Most students will score themselves honestly and accurately.

The DPS should count more than any other single measure toward the overall grade because it incorporates all the essential elements of high performance.

Benefits of the DPS

We have found it beneficial for students with an individualized education program (IEP) to have use of the DPS added to their IEP, so it becomes a requirement of their program that they take the DPS to each class and have the teacher fill it out. Filling out the DPS takes a few seconds and opens the door to meaningful dialogue about student performance. The scored sheets can then be provided to the case manager for evaluation.

In order for the DPS to make an impact on behavior, it must be faithfully filled out and addressed on a daily basis. If the teacher evaluates students' sheets daily, their feedback will have a significant impact on students who are disruptive and defiant. These students see immediately the impact their behavior is having on their performance and grade.

Individual Student Management Precepts

Individual student misbehavior can disrupt the learning environment. The following strategies are beneficial in managing individual student behavior. If strategies for managing the behavior of individual students are effectively planned prior to the beginning of class, the teacher will be in a good position to provide a quality learning experience for all students in the classroom.

Give and Take

We need to engage in a covert form of negotiation with difficult students. We might be willing to concede the daily assignment for 30 minutes of cooperation. We might be willing to offer a food or video coupon for 30 minutes of undisturbed study time. The trick is to avoid getting defiant students conditioned to getting a reward every time they behave in acceptable ways.

> **Remember This**
>
> Students are watching to see how you (fairly, lovingly, harshly, sarcastically) deal with disruptive students. Perception is their reality.

These students lack self-confidence and can be very manipulative. The teacher might reward a student errantly, and that is okay. It took this student a long time to develop these crafty skills, and it will take the teacher a long time to figure out the student's motivation and a strategy for controlling the situation.

Ask for an Apology

All individuals are moral agents. Students know right from wrong, but as we saw in Chapter 1, their definitions of right and wrong might vary from those of the classroom. The shift in social values, and the decline in human worth being taught through the media, require educators to strengthen their efforts to teach redeeming values in the classroom and school. Therefore, it is necessary to establish a moral standard for the classroom and reinforce the expectation through modeling and review. The teacher sets the standard and then enforces compliance through firm and fair consequences.

Asking a student to admit guilt is powerful. It has been our experience that a moral challenge (asking for an admission of guilt) is hard to implement, yet makes a much bigger impact on student behavior than punitive measures. Suggesting to defiant students that reduced consequences or a complete pardon can be offered when admission is given allows them the opportunity to self-correct. This demonstrates the desire of the teacher to assist in the moral development of the student. Students are still in control of their behavior; the only difference is that the teacher has reestablished the moral framework for it. This approach strikes at the heart of the behavior and addresses its root.

Setting an Example

Two things are human nature with youngsters: (1) they are willing to forgive and forget, and (2) most don't understand humility. It confuses them, and teaches them an important life skill when they see it practiced by adults. So you can set a powerful example by apologizing when you err yourself. Any miscalculated interaction with a defiant student should be addressed as soon as you are aware of the situation, and you should apologize (if necessary) as soon as possible. If you err during an intervention, things implode, and the class threatens mutiny, being humble can regain all that was lost. Sincerely and purposefully apologize, and move on.

> **Remember This**
>
> If the student complies and gets back on task, thank the student.

Reward the Positive

Students will work for rewards. Food coupons, computer time, Homework Savers (see Chapter 5), first in line for recess or lunch, trinkets, and gizmos all provide motivation. Setting expectations for rewards will result in improved student performance and an academically focused classroom environment. They can serve several purposes:

- They encourage introverted students to become more engaged.
- They encourage students to rise to higher levels of performance.
- When a student receives an award for a specific level of work, the reward helps set a standard for other students to strive for.

Rewards also encourage defiant and disruptive students to cooperate. These students are looking for acknowledgment and negative consequences, as that is what they are used to. When they receive positive reinforcement instead, they begin to pursue positive consequences, and behavior begins to improve. Sometimes rewarding disruptive students for minor improvement is just the intervention necessary for getting them moving in a constructive direction.

Tickets and Coupons

You can set up a system of awarding tickets, points, chips, tokens, or straws for on-task behavior or performing above and beyond expectations. Once a student collects a set amount (e.g., 50 tickets), the tickets can be exchanged for coupons obtained from local food establishments and stores. Creating an in-class store where students can buy things they want with tickets is another effective approach for rewarding student achievement. Or, at the end of each week, students can enter tickets into a raffle for a coupon or toy of choice. All these approaches encourage students to stay motivated and keep working and performing at their highest potential.

If you decide to use tickets as a reward for acceptable behavior, you should explain when you introduce the system that the tickets can be forfeited for inappropriate behavior. If a forfeit becomes necessary with an individual student, a private discussion about behavior and the need to remove rewards makes as big an impact as asking a student to write about the behavior. It is important for the student to *give* the reward back to you; you should never take the reward. It must be given willingly.

Use the Schedule

Lunch and Recess Detention

Sometimes it is useful to detain students after class to address behavior problems. This is a great time to get to know them on a personal level. Detention should last only long enough to address the issue and put corrective measures in place. Ten minutes is usually sufficient to revisit class standards, chart a course for improved behavior, and build rapport with the student. To drag out the detention becomes counterproductive and punitive, when the emphasis should be corrective.

Early Release to Lunch or Recess

Early release serves as a great motivator, either with an individual or with a whole class. Students who are allowed to leave 15 seconds early will be at the front of the lunch line. Be careful not to set yourself up by letting a student go early without the group understanding the rationale behind your decision: The early-departing student should set an example of performance that other students also have the opportunity to achieve.

Late Release to the Next Class

There are situations where having a student leave after the class has been dismissed will avoid potential problems during class transition. Late release does not usually require an escort, since the student has only one place to go, and all social distracters are in class. However, if the student still has trouble arriving at the next class, an escort might be necessary.

Derailing Disruptors

Respect for the teacher is gained or lost when a chronically disruptive student begins to act out. If the student is not dealt with in a timely manner, there is a good chance other students will begin to act out also, as they believe the teacher will not take action for unruly behavior. It is to the teacher's and the class's benefit that defiant and disruptive behavior be addressed as soon as it appears.

At the same time, it can be appropriate to ignore minor disruptions and instances of defiance and nonmotivation. It is critical for teachers to know their tolerance levels. Defiant and disruptive students are looking for what agitates the teacher. Ignoring minor attention-getting strategies (tapping pencils, clicking pens, bodily sounds) takes away the stage of the disruptive student. Such occasional minor disruptions should not be taken seriously.

> **Remember This**
>
> Chances are the other students in the class have been putting up with this disruptive behavior for several years. These students are more likely to ignore the behavior than the teacher.

> **Remember This**
>
> Never stop the lesson to address minor disruptions. Don't break your stride; keep teaching and marching forward.

Heading Off Disruptive Behavior

This section lists several approaches to dealing with disruptive behavior. The three tenets below can be applied to all of them.

- Students need to feel secure and validated.
- Tone of voice, a gentle touch, and sincere feelings communicate more than words.
- Peer pressure brings about the best in behavior choices.

Request Appropriate Contributions

The teacher should openly acknowledge inquisitive questions, comments, and suggestions. But if the commenting students are not on task, it is often helpful to address them by first name and ask them if they have something to contribute to the class or discussion. Timing and tact are critical. If you are going to regain the control the student just took, make sure you have eye contact with the student before you ask the question.

> ### Remember This
>
> There are no negotiations when a name is written on the board—only compliance. Students may negotiate after class. This must be clearly understood prior to implementation in order for this method to work. Student buy-in is not necessary, only understanding.

Write Students' Names on the Board

Getting disruptive students' attention is necessary for their own personal growth and to maintain class focus on what is important. Sometimes writing their names on the board can grab their attention.

Offer a Choice

Giving students a choice to make good decisions helps guide them toward making good decisions in the future, when their choices may be life changing. Let them know what the consequences will be for both good and bad decisions, and challenge them to consider the outcome of their choice. Students respond well to the following statement when a teacher is about to take action: "Don't make me do what I don't want to do." This comment opens the door to a discussion about who really is in charge of the outcome. They have been presented with their choices and are about to provide the teacher with directions as to what the teacher needs to do next. The comment really gets them to think about choices and consequences.

Defend Their Integrity

Defiant and disruptive students may try to use discussions of personal issues to derail class engagement. These students can be gently reminded of expectations that such issues are to be discussed out of class. The following tactful interventions can also be used to address these interruptions while avoiding embarrassment and maintaining student integrity:

- Caringly and tactfully ask the student, is there something wrong?
- Do you need to talk with a counselor?
- Let's wait until another time for that discussion.
- Class will be over soon. We can visit after class.
- Is this a life or death issue?

Note: Be careful with the last one. What is a life or death issue to a youngster (bad hair day, lost lunch money, disagreement with a friend or family member) is often vastly different from what is a life or death issue to an adult.

Remember This
Remind the disruptive student that personal concerns are to be discussed before school, during lunch, during recess, or after school.

Instructional Shifts

Using defiant students' own tactics can be helpful in maintaining control over their behavior. Keeping them off balance can prevent them from throwing the class off balance. A rapid pace will keep this type of student uncertain as to the teacher's emotional state, and an instructional shift can distract the student's plans to disrupt. For example, move the student unexpectedly to another area of the room where there is a better view of the lesson, or have the student work with a compliant student or group. Ask the student to collect or hand out papers. Finding anything to distract their disruptive behavior keeps them off balance and productive.

Isolate the Offender

For the chronic offender, it can be beneficial for them to work on an assignment in an isolated location. Be sure to check on isolated students every few minutes to assure them that they are not forgotten or unimportant.

Allow Time

With all interventions, give students an opportunity to self-adjust, and stop the intervention when there is evidence the students have learned the expected behavior. You will know this by watching their body language and hearing their comments; it may also be evident in their written statements. They might need a moment to get their mind in the right frame of thinking before they enter into the learning arena. By self-adjusting, students learn to limit their disruptions in the future.

Taking Up the Challenge If You Must

Despite your best efforts to treat students tactfully and respectfully, you must nevertheless be ready for the occasional rude comeback statement from a student, and be prepared to take up their challenge for classroom control. When the gauntlet is thrown down, you must be ready to pick it up. Don't argue. Some defiant students want to be sent to the office; however, they must learn to work with you. There is no easy way out.

A Statement That Shuts Down Confrontation

The following statement stops an assault on the teacher. "See me before school, at lunch or recess, or after school. This is instructional time." If the student wants to persist, turn your attention to the class and ask them to tell you when the times are for personal discussion or concerns. The class will respond in unison. This peer pressure usually ends the assault.

Proximity Is Intimidating

Walking into the disruptive student's area will usually cause them to stop the disruptive behavior, although it's best to enter a disruptive student's personal area *before* the disruptive behavior begins. Try to anticipate when they will become agitated. Seating them near your presentation station will facilitate this intervention.

Get down at the student's level or lower. If you know the student, kneeling works well. (If you don't know the student, or the student has a violent history, it is best to keep your distance—an arm's length is good—and stay on your feet if you need to move quickly.) Talk in a quiet voice, explaining the problem you're having. The student will generally respond in one of three ways:

1. Get embarrassed and apologize—this is the time to accept the apology and get back to instruction and learning.

2. Swear—if the swearword is spoken quietly, ignore it or confront it quietly.

3. Challenge—if the challenge is disruptive, the student should be reminded of when the appropriate time to challenge is (before school, at lunch or recess, after school), removed from the class, and given a Classroom Behavior Improvement Plan (see p. 46).

Additional Interventions for Addressing Challenges

Negotiate with unruly students. Everyone has a price. Find the win-win factor. Negotiation demonstrates benevolence, something with which most disruptive students have little experience. Explore options for when disruptive students may give input into their own consequences. Negotiating is a favorable solution with disruptive students; it gives them a chance to establish what they are willing to accept while not causing you to lose control of the situation.

If the student continues to be defiant and disruptive, he must be removed from the learning environment for the benefit of the other students. Do not engage in a discussion or respond to his comments or behaviors. Give your directive, and deal with him later, when the class is engaged in a learning activity.

Remind disruptive students that they don't have the right to take education away from other students, and that legal consequences can be imposed if they don't stop the defiance or leave the room. This approach is seldom used, and is a final option. (Check with your local juvenile prosecutor first and get the prosecutor's support before using this approach.)

The Redemption Plan

This is a plan for a whole class that combines several of the interventions we have discussed. It works best with highly social and active classes. The word *redemption* was attached to this process after it was introduced to a group of students who asked if they might get their names or checks by their names removed from the board if their behavior improved. Like all interventions, it has a positive component that encourages students to work toward improving their behavior.

The first step is to establish expectations for redemption:

Students will . . .

1. be in their seats when the bell rings.

2. have their folders out and be ready to work when the bell rings.

3. begin their assignments when the bell rings and continue to work throughout the period.

4. speak and act appropriately; there will be no swearing, vulgar talk, name calling, gestures of intimidation, or disturbing of others.

Negative consequences are then defined for instances of failure to meet expectations:

1st offense. Name on the board = Warning

2nd offense. Check by your name = Loss of tickets or points

3rd offense. Second check by your name = Lunch or recess detention

4th offense. Third check by your name = Removal from the class

At the same time, positive consequences are defined for improved behavior:

1. If a student behaves acceptably for 10 minutes, a check by that student's name will be removed.

2. Tickets will be awarded to students who follow the class expectations.

3. Students who have not had their names added to the board may be allowed to leave early for lunch.

For the class, there can also be a positive group consequence:

If there are no names on the board at the end of class, the teacher will hold a raffle, release the class early, or award extra tickets to all students.

Knowing When to Push the Ejection Button

Comments targeted at the teacher, open defiance, rudeness, swearing, and aggression are all reasons for removing a student from the classroom. Students can be allowed to reenter the learning environment when they have completed a statement defining what they did to disrupt the learning process and what their plan is to avoid the behavior in the future (see p. 46). Until students admit to what they did and come up with a plan of how they are going to avoid the same behavior in the future, repeat performances will take place.

The following methods are suggested as stopgap measures only, and are not intended for everyday use. Consistent enforcement of classroom expectations will eliminate the need for them.

Time-Out

Some students need a break to get refocused on the lesson or to remember why they are in school. Sending a student to a time-out station, in an adjacent classroom or isolated seat, allows disruptions to be cut short and instructional time to be maximized.

Student-Initiated Removal From the Room

Rare moments occur when students will ask for a quiet place to study when the classroom will not work for their academic needs. When a trusted student makes a request to work in the hallway or to go to the library, it is in the teacher's best interest to honor the student's desire. Ignoring the suggestion without explanation could lead to defiance. Students who make such a request show an awareness of their emotional state, and their desire to resolve possible classroom disruptions should be honored. This approach will gain the student's trust, and may make the student an ally in future efforts to manage the class.

Placing a Student in the Hall

When all attempts to refocus disruptive students have failed, removal to the hallway or another quiet place is necessary to maintain control of the learning environment and to keep the lesson moving forward. This puts them in an environment where they can reflect on their behavior. It also gives them the control they were looking for, but the teacher has defined parameters for appropriate behavior.

When you place students in the hallway, tell them,

1. When you can tell me what you did, then you can rejoin the class.

2. What will you do to avoid this situation from happening again?

3. Let me know when you are ready to talk.

Check on students in the hall every five minutes. If needed, have a paraprofessional or aide sit with them. Allow students to reenter the learning environment when they have filled out a Classroom Behavior Improvement Plan or had a one-on-one conference with you. If they choose the latter, documentation of the conference is recommended.

One-on-one discussions take away the audience disruptive students want. One-on-one time also gets to the heart of the issue and gives students a platform to explain their concerns. Many misunderstandings have been resolved in personal discussions.

Using Out of Class Time Effectively

Classroom Behavior Improvement Plan (CBIP)

This strategy is effective in causing defiant and disruptive students to reflect on their behavior through cognitive and written processing. It forces students to address their behavior before they are allowed back into the learning environment. The written component of this process imprints the experience in the student's mind and provides documentation for future follow-up. The strategy can be used by a single teacher, between cooperating teachers, or schoolwide.

Preparation

To prepare, create and make copies of a CBIP form like the form shown in Figure 3.2. You must also establish a refocus or time-out station, either in your classroom or under the supervision of a colleague elsewhere. If the station is in your classroom, it is suggested it be established toward the back of the classroom to avoid giving undue attention to the disruptive student. In a situation where teachers share adjacent rooms, it is effective to have the disruptive student leave the room and report to the cooperating teacher's room. At the refocus station there should be additional CBIP forms in case students lose theirs or need to start over.

The Process

1. Place the misbehaving student's name on the board as a warning that he or she is at risk of being sent to the refocus station.

2. If the disruptive behavior persists, give a CBIP form to the disruptive student, who is to report directly to the refocus station and complete the form.

3. The student goes to the refocus station or another teacher's room.

4. Upon the student's return, have the student place the CBIP in a prearranged place that will cause minimal distraction to the class.

process their responses, completing the loop. Finally, they verbally defend their responses to the teacher, and we hope they commit to their solutions for avoiding a repeat of the behavior.

This process serves several purposes. First, the student must recognize and address the issue. Second, the teacher has a written record to add to the student's portfolio and refer to if future concerns arise. Finally, there is documentation supporting the teacher's attempt to correct the behavior.

Having students write out what their disruptive behaviors are and formulating plans for avoiding the poor behavior in the future will decrease the chances of the behavior happening again.

5. Confirm the student's value as a class member as the student is reinstalled as an active class participant, prepared to follow the CBIP plan and class expectations.

5. Follow up with the student in writing or discussion. Not all students are capable of having a productive discussion upon returning from the refocus station. It might be better to write a follow-up comment to the student or wait for a calm period before having a discussion.

Note: We have had cases where this process takes place multiple times with the same student, and each time a new plan is written. This is not an exercise in futility, as you will see incremental changes taking place.

Figure 3.2   Classroom Behavior Improvement Plan

Name:

Date:

Period:

Class Title:

Directions:

- Answer each of the following carefully and thoughtfully.
- When finished, return to the classroom.
- Place the CBIP on the teacher's desk.
- Return to your seat and follow your plan.

1. In your own words, describe what happened.

   _____

   _____

   _____

   _____

2. How could you have responded differently?

   _____

   _____

   _____

   _____

3. What is your plan to prevent this from happening again?

   _____

   _____

   _____

   _____

4. Why is your plan a good plan?

   _____

   _____

   _____

   _____

Considerations for Allowing a Student to Return to the Classroom

It is important that the teacher maintains control of the student's return, and allows it only when the student has provided an acceptable response. This is a delicate matter. If the student believes she or he has complied with the expectation, it becomes vital (for the health of the relationship between student and teacher) that this intervention be perceived as corrective and not punitive. The teacher's timing and presentation to the returning student are critical. The situation could escalate and the relationship deteriorate, causing additional instances of disruption, if the teacher is in a reactive mode. In other words, the teacher needs to stay focused on correcting the behavior through student compliance, not submission.

Students who insist they have complied when the teacher disagrees should be moved to a seat outside the direct learning environment to avoid further contamination of the learning process, and be reminded that they may return when they are ready to behave acceptably. The teacher should not debate with them, but simply remove them again to the refocus station and return to teaching. They may return to the learning environment after they have completed an acceptable CBIP and when the teacher believes they are capable of rejoining the class without drawing undue attention to themselves.

If the teacher does not feel the student should return without further counsel, then during a lull in the class period, the teacher can visit with the student privately and ask for an explanation of what led to the student's removal. If the student wants to continue the debate, the teacher should leave the student, explaining that she or he will return later to see if the student has an answer. Teachers should never allow themselves to be drawn into a debate.

> **Remember This**
>
> It took many years for the student to learn these behaviors, and it is going to take many more attempts to reverse the process. Keep the focus. Teachers have approximately five hours a day at the elementary level and one or possibly two hours at the secondary level to make changes, over a nine-month period.
>
> After school hours, weekends, and vacations skew the ratio in favor of the student's out-of-school experiences to in-school experiences. Hence, it is vital to explain to the students that what is expected in their homes can be vastly different from what is expected in the classroom.

> **Remember This**
>
> Your response could either build the relationship or alienate the student. The approach you choose will determine the future of your effectiveness with the student.

Remember This

Some students will want to discuss the issue. They need to be reminded that this is not a discussion. Discussion can happen after class. This is about their admission of wrong, and readmission to the class.

Remember This

Students must own their behavior before they can control it.

If the student is not willing to acknowledge inappropriate behavior, it is a good idea to have the student write down an answer anyway. Teachers should try to preserve the students' right to be angry in this situation. The student is probably not angry with the teacher; rather, the teacher is the convenient target for an unresolved issue that took place outside the classroom.

If a student reluctantly provides adequate answers on the CBIP form, the teacher should provide clear directions of the behavior expected upon return to the class and have the student paraphrase what is expected. Students who refuse to paraphrase are not ready to return. The issue has now changed to defiance.

Let's Try That Again

Some students need to stay outside the learning environment until they are ready to comply with class expectations. Having the defiant student fill out a CBIP is critical for behavior modification. Until disruptive students are willing to admit they are wrong and provide steps for how they are going to improve their behavior, they should not be allowed back into the learning environment.

Although the CBIP process may seem at first to require an enormous amount of effort, the effort pays off in improved behavior in the classroom. Figure 3.3 shows the drop in disruptive incidents in our classroom over a seven-month period when the CBIP process was in use. Observe how student misbehavior increased from October to September, and then went into a consistent decline over the next five months. An increase in misbehavior is typical and expected when a new management plan is put in place. The teacher must not back away from the plan.

In-School Suspension

Keeping students at school and under strict guidelines for behavior serves as an intervention for students who are delayed in their social development. Sending students home is not going to allow for the type of intervention the student needs. Keeping

Figure 3.3   Decline in Disruptive Incidents Over Seven Months

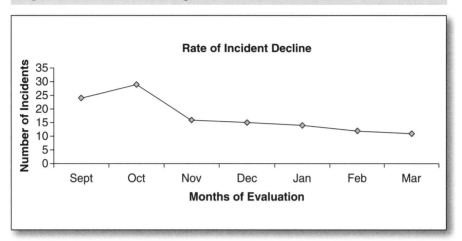

suspended students isolated from the rest of the student population provides time for them to reflect and receive additional training in expected social interaction.

Schools that do not have the means for a separate in-school suspension room can solicit teachers for their room use. We have seen this system work effectively with one student being assigned to a cooperating teacher for the course of the school day. These students are provided assignments and behavior interventions. Lunch is also provided in isolation. None of the other students should be allowed to engage with the suspended student. When using this approach, we have found it best to have the suspension station located in the back of the classroom and facing the wall, or in a cubicle.

Carding Disruptive Behavior

This intervention requires prior knowledge about soccer rules and the consequences of penalties when rules are violated. When introducing this strategy, first ask the class for a show of hands of those who are familiar with the rules of soccer. Most students know someone who has played soccer. Second, ask the class for a volunteer who can tell the class what a yellow card in soccer means. Then ask, "Are players still allowed in the game after they receive a yellow card?" Repeat the same sequence for the red card.

Inform the class that penalty cards will be presented for violation of class rules. Discussion about receiving a card can only happen before school, at lunch, at recess, or after school. The consequences for being presented each card are as follows:

- yellow card = lunch or recess detention and a CBIP for violation of class rules
- red card = removal from the class and CBIP prior to reentry for violation of class rules

Note that a red card removes students from the immediate class setting and puts them in the refocus station until a CBIP is completed satisfactorily.

Below is an example of what could be written on a card.

> **Academic Violation.** Your behavior has made a negative impact on your education and your classmates. Your behavior may result in removal from the class. In the event you are removed, readmission to the class will be allowed only when you successfully complete a CBIP. No discussion about this card will take place in class. Discussion may take place between 7:30 AM and 7:45 AM; during lunch period or recess, or from 3:00 PM to 3:15 PM.

Strategies for Using the Class to Manage Individual Students

Remember This

Children have their own way of thinking about values, so the correct way to view the child is as a moral philosopher. (Lawrence Kolhberg)

The pure joy for teaching emerges when students start to hold each other accountable and operate as self-starters. This is easier to achieve at the younger levels (K–5) and in block instructional settings where teacher and students work together for extended periods of time. When students move from one teacher to another, as often occurs at the secondary level, it is much harder to maintain operational continuity.

Disruptive students facing their peers will begin to observe that their behavior is not acceptable even among their classmates. It's one thing to expect adults to take offense at defiant and disruptive behavior; however, when fellow students hold each other accountable, they create an environment in which personal accountability and self-management are required of each student. This strategy sets up a system in which students can hold each other accountable.

Peer Accountability—Grades K–4

Setup

The teacher awards each student 10 points at the beginning of each day. Points are awarded during an opening ceremony along with other opening activities. This celebrates hope for every student and honors every child.

The class decides which infractions will result in the loss of points. Infractions might include being unkind, out of line, too loud, unsafe, or unfair. For clarity, the teacher should teach or role-play what each of the infractions looks like. One to five points can be deducted per violation.

Behavior Intervention Process

After a group activity (recess or lunch), the teacher announces, "Accountability Report," and calls on each student by name to report on classmate behavior. Every student gives a report, saying either "no report" or giving a student's name and announcing only what the student did that is on the deduction list; for example, "Bobby, being unkind." The named student stands and repeats "being unkind" or says "explain."

When asked to explain, the reporting student gives a short report on what happened. The accused student then has a second chance to accept the accusation for fewer lost points. If the accused student still refuses to admit the offense, the teacher rules on the amount of points the accused student is to lose. If a second reporting student makes the same accusation against the same accused student, the accused student loses the maximum points (five).

> **Remember This**
>
> Students talk to everybody. A teacher's best allies can be students. When they get alone with their peers, they can take a stand for the teacher's policies and decisions, and this can work to correct errant students' behavior. Students care about what their peers think and will comply with expectations when peers challenge the disruptive behavior.

> **Remember This**
>
> Admission of guilt is the first stage in healing a relationship.

The teacher keeps track of who has lost how many points on a record sheet for the teacher's eyes only. Students who have not lost points by the end of the week are recognized and rewarded by the teacher.

Class Court—Grades 4–8

This concept was created for an eighth grade math teacher who had several students who were disrupting and controlling the teacher's instructional time. The genius of this strategy is that the disrupting students take ownership for their behavior. It puts these students on center stage as they develop the process with the class. What makes this strategy effective is that the students creating and introducing the process are the ones who are being targeted for behavior improvement.

Setup

The teacher meets with the disruptive group outside of class time, perhaps during the teacher's planning time, to present and establish the court concept. The disruptive group creates two lists of consequences: one for a not guilty plea (e.g., lunch detention, phone call to parents, implementation of the 24-hour rule [see p. 57]), and one for a guilty plea (e.g., apologize to the class, fill out a CBIP, go to the refocus station, clean up the room). The consequences for a not guilty plea should be greater than the consequences for a guilty plea. To create ownership, the process is designed and presented to the class by the most disruptive students.

Behavior Intervention Process

The offending student is quietly confronted by the teacher and given a choice between facing the teacher's consequence or facing the class court. A defending student or defending student's selected representative presents the case to the class in one minute or less. The list of possible consequences is written on the board or presented on a poster so all students can see the list. The class votes on a verdict and a consequence, using a ballot like the one shown on page 55. Votes are kept secret, and the class returns to work.

The teacher evaluates the ballots while the class is working and presents the verdict privately to the student at the end of class. Providing the verdict at the end of class avoids confrontations.

Sample Class Court Ballot

Directions: Check your verdict and a consequence from the list on the board.

_____Guilty

Selected Consequence (select from list)

_____
_____

_____Not Guilty

Selected Consequence (select from list)

_____
_____

Additional Allies in the Effort to Improve Individual Behavior

School Staff and Community Members

Use your aides, parents, and teaching assistants for correcting papers, recording points, Internet searches, copying, filing, and tutoring. Use their gifts well. These individuals observe the classroom from a different point of view than you do. You can learn from their perspectives.

In addition, various other individuals are helpful in assisting the teacher with difficult students.

Classified Staff

Custodians are great for keeping rooms orderly and clean. Getting and keeping them on the teacher's side is helpful in meeting classroom needs. They can also be useful in counseling students, as they do not present themselves as authority figures.

True Encounter

Sebastian was a Latino student who did not want to be in the United States and was angry with his parents for taking him away from his grandfather's farm in Mexico. Sebastian knew English but refused to speak or

(Continued)

(Continued)

write it. During class he consistently engaged in Spanish conversations with other Latino students. It seemed the efforts of the teacher only resulted in Sebastian increasing his efforts to resist. It was eventually discovered that he was trying to start a gang movement, and speaking Spanish was a cover-up for his activities, as the teacher did not know Spanish.

The teacher contacted the custodian, who was Latino, and asked him to talk with Sebastian, in Spanish, and explain what was expected in class and the consequences for disruptive behavior. Sebastian was surprised that the teacher had made the effort to reach out to him in Spanish through the custodian.

The bond between the custodian, the teacher, and Sebastian held Sebastian in check, because he knew that the teacher had the custodian as an ally. A Spanish-speaking paraprofessional's support also allowed the teacher to gain information about what Sebastian was saying, because Sebastian did not know the paraprofessional knew Spanish. When she heard something about which she was concerned, she reported to the teacher, who would then confront Sebastian.

These efforts kept Sebastian off guard and confused as to how the teacher was able to communicate with him in English and Spanish. Sebastian eventually stopped defiantly speaking in Spanish and followed a rule the teacher gave him for using it. He was allowed to use Spanish only for clarification of instructions with other students.

Probation Officers

Legal authorities have tremendous leverage with the students involved with the correctional system. When the teacher collects probation officers' phone numbers (see Chapter 1) and visits with officers who come to counsel parolees, it informs disruptive and defiant students that their teacher is actively involved with their discipline outside the school setting as well as within it.

Student Resource Officers

Local police officers assigned to the school are a valuable source of legal and community knowledge. They are often connected with the students and their environment. When teachers talk to their students about the resource officer, students realize the teacher has avenues of addressing their behavior beyond those in the school setting.

School Administrators

In-house support is always helpful, but administrators should be the last people teachers call for help. Their days are full. The methods found on these pages should be implemented before administrators are involved. The principal is a support base, not the classroom disciplinarian.

Working With Parents

There are a variety of ways to work with parents to improve student behavior. Any time contact with home is made, the student should receive prior notice. Much trust is lost if a student's parent or guardian is notified of defiant behavior without the student's knowledge. In addition, students may become angry if their parents are contacted without their being informed, and this can cause further classroom disruption.

Conference Call With Student to Parent or Guardian

A conference call is a great way for students to share with their parents or guardians without having to look them in the eye. There is something about preserving personal integrity that gives the student confidence to share when the parent is not physically present. The teacher also benefits by being able to hear what the student and parent are talking about.

Setting up this process carefully is vital. First, the student must agree to the conference call. Students must be given the option of just listening to the conversation between the teacher and the parent, but they must understand that if they tell their parents about the problem first—before the parents hear about it from the teacher—things may be easier for them at home. If they choose to talk to their parents first, students must inform the parent that the teacher is listening. Finally, students must understand that the teacher will talk to the parents only if the parents desire.

The 24-Hour Rule

Getting defiant and disruptive students to face their errors is paramount to behavior change. They must address the issue personally before change can begin. They will resist the process until they realize the academic process will be on hold until they cooperate with class expectations. The 24-hour rule opens the door for difficult students to take ownership of what they have been doing to disrupt their learning and that of others.

The rule works like this: When students disrupt the learning process and the parents must be called, students can be given 24 hours to talk to their parents before the call is made. Within 24 hours, at a convenient time, students must tell their parents about the disruptive behavior. They may do this whenever they think the discussion will be best received, as long as it's within 24 hours. Parents must call the teacher after they hear about the offense from the students, and students must bring a signed note from home documenting the confession. If students do not tell their parents within 24 hours, the teacher initiates the call to parents.

Like the conference call above, this gives students an opportunity to tell their parents first, before the parents hear about the infraction from the teacher.

Informing Parents by E-mail

Some parents want to be notified as soon as their student misbehaves. When an e-mail address is available, the teacher can draft an e-mail to parents about a disruptive incident while the class is working, and then invite the disruptive student to the computer to review what the teacher has written. This is particularly effective if the teacher allows students to think they are getting away with defiant behavior while the teacher is writing the e-mail, explaining each detail as it is happening.

As with any contact with home, the student must be informed before the "send" button is pushed. What we have found works best is to have the student understand that the teacher can send the message, or the student can be invited to send it.

If the teacher feels the point has been made, and the student's behavior has improved, the teacher might agree to place the e-mail in an archive for future use. Sometimes the student needs to be reminded about the e-mail and that it can be updated if necessary. Keeping a running list of dated occurrences in an unsent e-mail can be very effective. Letting students know that the list can be sent to their parents or the school office at any time usually gets defiant and disruptive students back on track. Providing them a copy of the list is also effective in making the point that action is imminent.

We have noticed that when students send such an e-mail message, an improvement in their behavior occurs. It's as if they have evoked the wrath of their parents, understanding that consequences will follow at home. But be sure to make back-up copies of all e-mails sent. Some students are technologically capable, and they have been known to delete a message at home before their parents read it.

Electronic Referrals

There are many electronic discipline programs available. All of them provide power to the teacher. One of the most effective tools we have found is the e-referral. E-referrals can be prepared and forwarded to administration, parents, and staff the moment defiant behavior surfaces. In addition to the formats available through electronic discipline programs, e-referral forms can be created using a word processing program, filled out with the details of disruptive behavior, and distributed via a shared electronic folder, a listserv, or e-mail. Creating an electronic folder for e-referrals allows for efficient cataloging of student behavior.

It is effective to allow the student to read the referral and respond to the account that has been recorded. Once the student has a clear understanding of the behavior problem and the referral's contents, the teacher can send the referral, or give the student the option to send it. When a student sends the referral, the action creates a form of confession by the student.

Informing Parents by Cell Phone

Most parents appreciate personal contact with teachers. Using this mode of communication provides for faster input and direction. Students use cell phones to inform parents about teacher behavior, and teachers can use this technology too to keep parents informed about positive and disruptive behaviors.

True Encounters

These two encounters illustrate the power of the use of cell phones.

A student was upset with the actions of her teacher regarding a dress code violation. The teacher was unaware that the student had sent a text message

(Continued)

(Continued)

to her parent. Moments later the classroom door opened, and there stood the parent. It was as if the parent had materialized in the room. The teacher, student, and parent met in the hallway to discuss the student's clothing. The parent was upset that her daughter had changed out of the clothes she was wearing when she left home. The parent apologized for the disturbance and took the child home.

A teacher was having a difficult time with the class and began to shout and became profane. A student secretly called her parent from the classroom. Moments later, the classroom door opened, and the parent and the principal were standing in the doorway. The teacher was removed from the classroom and placed on administrative leave.

Technology is powerful.

Process and Apply

1. Outline the documentation process you are currently using.

2. List three significant outcomes your documentation process is having on behavior.

3. Create or modify a documentation strategy that will work with your particular class and grade level.

4. Design a DPS that fits your own classroom situation.

5. Create a CBIP form that meets your student management needs.

6. Outline a student incentives program to include what incentives you would use and how you would apply them.

7. How could intercepting defiant behavior be a good strategy for containing disruptive behavior before it has a chance to get started?

8. Outline a strategy for using e-mail, e-referrals, and cell phones to help manage student behavior.

4

Strategies for Managing Classroom Behavior

An emergency staff meeting was called to address what to do with Isaac, a socially delayed 15-year-old. Many of his behaviors are those of a 9- or 10-year-old. Isaac enjoys drawing attention to himself, and he has no regard for the threat to his personal safety posed by other students hoping to find a way to stop his annoying behavior.

Having sat in the meeting long enough to hear each teacher's concerns, it became evident to me that they had no plan for dealing with Isaac's disruptive behavior. It was at that point that I decided to take up the challenge of being Isaac's personal mentor. Most of the strategies listed within these pages were useful for curbing Isaac's behavior.

The results were encouraging. Within the first week, Isaac reduced his disruptive behavior by 90%. This was largely because he and I had one-on-one discussions outside the learning environment, and we planned how to be successful. The essence of the plan was to have Isaac sent to my room by the other teachers as soon as his behavior became disruptive. With Isaac's assistance, a modified DPS was created, and he took it around to each of his teachers on a daily basis. He had a target score that he met occasionally; for this, he was rewarded with a fast food coupon of his choice. As his behavior and performance continued to improve, his target score was increased. When Isaac fell behind on assignments, he was escorted to my room for lunchtime study hall, where he ate his lunch and completed assignments.

The progressive strategies mentioned here produced the results we desired. Students stopped threatening bodily harm to Isaac. Classroom disruptions were greatly reduced, and academic performance improved. Managing the classroom behavior of Isaac also created a managed and healthy learning environment for all the students.

The newest curriculum and instructional methods are not the magical answer for getting students to be productive. Making sure students have a safe and manageable learning environment is what enables teachers to teach the curriculum as intended. Structure and atmosphere are the first lessons. Instruction will be limited until the learning environment is well managed.

Ninety-nine percent of teachers new to the profession have not received a course in classroom management. Most of the undergraduate coursework focuses on academic lesson plans and curriculum. Students understand what the content of the class will be. What students expect the teacher to do is establish a calm and focused learning environment. Hence, classroom structure must be established first.

To help assess the learning environment in their classrooms, there are several important questions teachers should ask. The answers to these questions identify how students perceive the classroom:

1. Is the classroom safe, emotionally and physically?

2. Do students come to the classroom seeking comfort and security?

3. Do students stop by to visit?

4. Do students want to have lunch in the classroom?

It is the answers to these questions that reveal how students perceive the care of the teacher and the safety of the classroom. This next step in our journey to successful student management will help teachers create a classroom environment that enables teachers to answer "yes" to these questions.

Establishing a Good Learning Environment

Managing Your Behavior to Help Students Manage Theirs

The first contact in the classroom is visual. Students observe and ask themselves, is the teacher friendly, controlling, or benevolent? They check out the teacher first, the room second, and last, who is in the room, usually because they already know who is in the class. It is the nonverbal communication that becomes the first instruction of the class.

If you greet students as they enter the classroom, it lets them know you care about your classroom and want to provide the best for them. If you constantly yell at students or teach in an elevated voice, it creates an atmosphere of tension. If, instead, you create a calm atmosphere, students will have a greater tendency to get focused on learning, and the chances that they will maintain their focus are greatly increased.

Be a Listener

Active listening to student concerns is critical. If students feel they have a say in class operations, they are more likely to accept changes in operational standards. Students respond best when teachers write down student input. When a teacher offers a constructive response, student and teacher collaboration is more likely.

Invite, Encourage, and Solicit Interaction

Interaction can be difficult to obtain, especially with introverted youngsters. Building trust is the goal. Getting students engaged can be accomplished through various means: calling on students, taking turns, random selection, and bribery.

Before any significant interaction can take place, you must establish that the classroom is a safe place to share openly. Once you have achieved that, stepping aside and giving the students the stage can be effective. Students expect you to be the orator; therefore, it is a powerful strategy to give them the first opportunity to share. Again, being a listener and then paraphrasing what was said invites interaction. This empowers the students and sets the standard that everyone participates.

Remain in Charge

In a good learning environment, there is no misunderstanding about who is in charge. Student power brokers need to be dealt with the moment they start to challenge authority. If groups of students desire to derail the lesson and disrupt the learning process, you need to separate them the first time they disrupt.

Avoid Opportunistic Twists of Your Assignments or Words

Youngsters are opportunists. Give them an opening and they will run toward it. If it is within the lesson design to give students some latitude in how they will complete an assignment, be prepared for what the students might do with the freedom.

Some good ideas and outcomes have come from allowing students to explore new information. Often the best learning comes from student ownership in what they have designed. On the other hand, defiant students will use this opportunity for counterproductive ends and additional disruptions. Therefore, if the students are going to be allowed to work independent of the teacher's direct instruction, it is best to match disruptive students with students who are focused and task oriented.

Remember This

Be aware of and anticipate what students can do with your efforts. We live in a culture that feeds on innuendos. Monitor what you are going to say. Students, even the cooperative ones, have been conditioned to twist and read into what is said.

Similarly, you might get blindsided by students when you use what you believe to be a harmless statement. In the students' culture, the statement might mean something totally different (often sexual or demeaning) from what it means to you. To avoid such opportunistic misinterpretations, keep up-to-date on what the latest words, phrases, symbols, gestures, and behaviors are in youth culture. Teachers have been the brunt of a joke and increased class disruption out of ignorance about the culture of students they work with. The safest thing to do is to maintain a high intellectual vocabulary and avoid euphemisms.

Know Your Limits

Being consistent is vital to class control. The ability to maintain composure is necessary in order for students to be able to predict what the boundaries are. When disruptive students know their teacher is reaching a boiling point, it can work against the teacher. Sometimes it becomes a game to see how fast they can get the teacher to lose control. Therefore, knowing when you are reaching the limits of what you will tolerate is good personal management that benefits the class.

Students know their disruptive classmates intimately, better than the teacher. Many of them have played sports, live in the same neighborhood, hunted, or hung out together for years, and they know who the difficult students are. The only question remaining is how the teacher is going to handle their disruptive classmate. Will you treat the student with respect? Your interaction with this student will inform the others of how they might be handled also.

Grace is defined as respite or rest. Don't let them push your buttons. Take a deep breath, relax, and you will live to teach another day. It's best to simmer until you can take a moment (recess or lunch) to work through what happened, why, and what can be done to avoid the situation in the future.

It is also wise never to take a student's actions personally. Do all you can to maintain the student's dignity, and attempt to find out the underlying cause of the disruptive behavior. Success comes from knowing your students, their strengths, and their weaknesses.

> **Remember This**
>
> Don't overreact or allow your buttons to be pushed. It's when you want to explode—and don't—that personal growth takes place and student respect is earned. Students know when they have crossed the line and are waiting to see how you will react.

Using Seat Assignments to Manage Your Class

Choice of seat is a luxury, not a right. When students misbehave, they forfeit the luxury of choosing their seats. Seating assignments can be altered when the teacher feels there is a need for refocusing on learning. Placing difficult students in assigned seats helps control disruptive behavior.

It is not recommended that each student have an assigned seat. Only students who refuse or have demonstrated that they are unable to make appropriate decisions should be assigned a seat. We have discovered that when mutiny is on the horizon, students should be made to sit in assigned seats.

Chronically tardy students should be assigned a seat away from the other students. This response impacts the disruptive student's desire to be with friends. When chronically tardy students begin to be on time and engaged, they may gain the opportunity to sit with friends.

Students who perform well at an assigned seat should be provided the opportunity to sit where they want. Short periods outside the assigned seat for movie viewing or working on group assignments are good ways to earn your confidence that they can reenter the main seating area. Time away from an assigned seat is helpful and serves as a test of a student's integrity and ability to manage behavior.

It is recommended that a refocus station also be set up in isolation as a temporary CBIP station (see Chapter 3). These seats should be established toward the back of the classroom to minimize distractions.

Seating Facing a Wall

Youngsters thrive on attention, and when isolated they are willing to do almost anything to get back into the group setting. We have found when a student's assigned seat is against a wall, facing away from the general population, the student is more focused on the lesson. Sometimes a student will send notes, mouth comments, make faces, or send text messages, and it is at this point that the student needs to have all visual distractions removed. Hence, the student is directed to turn her or his desk toward the wall for a given period of time. Ten minutes of productive work results in the student being granted the right to turn the desk back toward the class.

> **Remember This**
>
> Failure to inform students of the consequences for defiant behavior invites a firestorm and class disruption. Walk them through the expectations and steps that will be taken for compliant and noncompliant behavior.

Figure 4.1 shows a sample seating chart that can be used with students at any grade level.

Figure 4.1   Individual Seat Assignments (K–12)

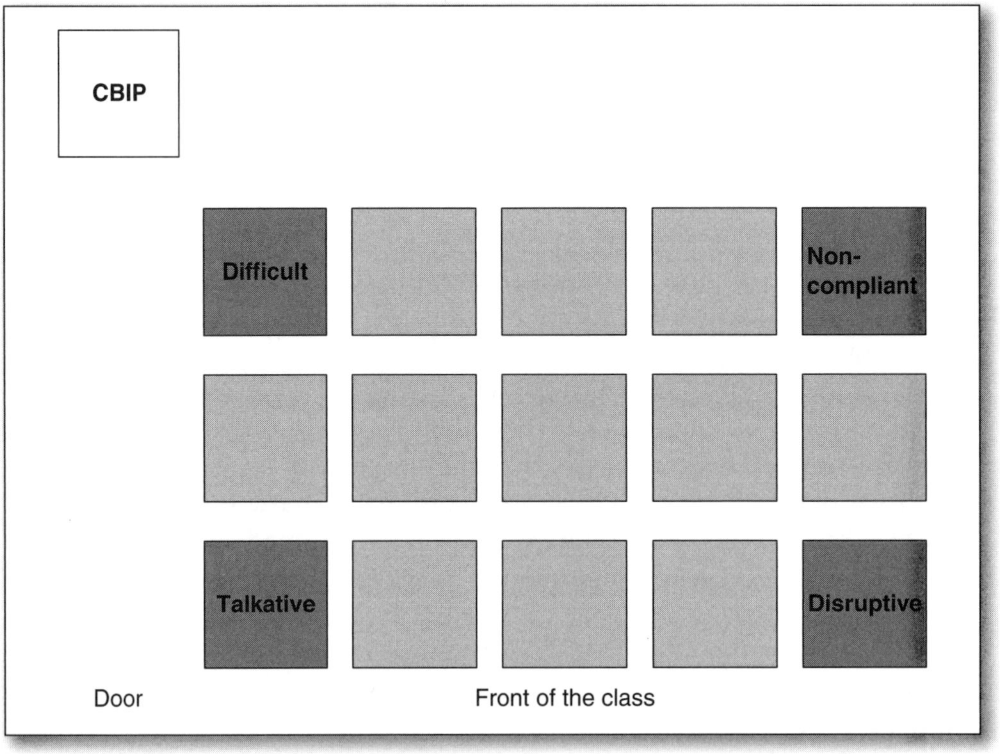

Source: www.pioneereducationconsulting.com

Allowing Students to Be Out of Their Seats

Roaming and standing in designated areas of the classroom can give students a constructive option for monitoring their own behavior. If a student has not gained the trust of the teacher, the student might be required to ask permission before getting out of the seat.

Helping Students to Dress for Success

Teachers often find it difficult to confront youngsters about their clothing. The following document makes this process as nonengaging as possible. The teacher gives the slip to the student. The student follows the directions on the slip, and the issue is resolved without discussion.

Dress Code Violation Notification Notice

Student: _____ Time: _____

You are currently in violation of the student dress code. You need to quietly remove yourself from the class and go to the office. If you have clothing to put on that will fix this problem, please take it with you to the office. Please check in with one of the staff members listed below.

Secretary: _____ Assistant Principal: _____ Principal: _____

Source: Prosser High School Handbook, Prosser, WA.

A Sample Clothing Policy

Policy: Clothing that may be considered gang-related or advocating violence or that displays inappropriate language, sexual innuendo, or advertisements for drugs, alcohol, or tobacco is prohibited. Clothing shall not be excessively tight, revealing, or distracting; see-through clothing may not be worn. Undergarments shall not be visible, including, but not limited to, any part of a bra (including the straps) or boxer shorts or the elastic waistband of underwear.

Tops: Tops shall completely cover the torso (the stomach and lower back) at all times. No cleavage shall be visible at any time. Unacceptable tops include, but are not limited to, the following: halter tops, off-the-shoulder

(Continued)

(Continued)

tops, bare-midriff tops, and fishnet tops. Sleeveless tops and tank tops shall not have extremely large armholes that will unnecessarily expose undergarments or bare skin.

Pants: Sagging or the wearing of pants or shorts below the waist and in a manner that allows underwear or bare skin to show, and bagging, or the wearing of excessively baggy pants or shorts with low-hanging crotches, are prohibited.

Skirts and Shorts: Skirts, shorts, and skorts shall not be shorter than midthigh (standing and sitting). If skirts, shorts, or skorts have a slit, the top of the slit shall not go over midthigh (standing and sitting).

Source: Prosser High School Handbook, Prosser, WA.

Entry Activities as a Management and Instructional Tool

Remember This
When the student body is informed of a policy change, the effectiveness of the intervention is determined by how much the teacher wants to put up with in enforcing it. A policy is only effective if it is enforced.

Students have a tendency to gravitate toward social behavior and away from academic focus when they are not managed under a standard set of expectations. Use of a daily entry activity, usually relating to the prior day's lesson, is a good way to establish the tone for the lesson. The entry activity allows for several key functions to take place. Individual entry activities are effective in getting the students focused. Individual work reduces side conversations and minimizes continued dialogue from the hallway. From the moment the entry task is revealed, students are engaged, and this creates a studious atmosphere. Entry activities have numerous other advantages as well.

Entry Activities Reduce Tardiness

Students engaged with the lesson before the tardy bell rings establish a standard for disruptive students who arrive after the tardy bell. The standard "being early is on time, and being on time is late" has a unique effect: Students will begin to think they are late when they arrive in class and classmates are already engaged with the lesson, even if the tardy bell has not yet rung. With the expectation that class begins the moment the student enters the room, attendance issues diminish.

In addition, while students are working on the entry activity, the teacher has time to address attendance concerns, such as dealing with tardy students, daily attendance taking, and catching up with students who are returning from illness, suspension, or vacations.

Entry Activities Reduce Disruptive Behavior

Entry activities automatically reduce defiant behavior, as students become accustomed to what needs to be done. When students enter a classroom that has reliable and consistent expectations of what is needed to succeed and the materials to obtain success, valuable learning can take place, and faster engagement with the lesson takes place. The entry activity causes the students to focus on academics, and there is little time for defiant and disruptive behavior to occur. A busy mind won't have time to think of how to disrupt the learning process.

Many defiant and disruptive behaviors can be squelched at the door when this trend is established on a daily basis. Teachers should listen for innuendos, volatile subject content, personal information, and unnecessary controversies as students come in the door and address it independently while the other students complete the entry activity.

An essential element of the entry activity for defiant and disruptive students is a time constraint for completing the activity. The activity should take no more than five minutes for all students. (The proportion of the activity completed by students on an IEP or 504 plan should be evaluated according to their plans.) Keeping the students informed of the remaining time, by calling out the time, creates necessary guidance for defiant and disruptive students.

Entry Activities Provide Opportunities for Review and Reinforcement

Entry activities also provide a perfect segue into the day's lesson. Review from the day before brings about clarifying questions left hanging from the previous day. Reconnecting students with yesterday's lesson is vital in preparing for the upcoming lesson for the day. Connecting past learning to the present strengthens the knowledge base necessary for mastery of the subject.

Remember This

The entry activity is a review of yesterday's lesson. It is not the introduction of new information. The entry task could be looked upon as a daily assessment.

Once the entry task is collected, the correct answers should be provided. Review of the entry task, with the class, provides additional emphasis on the learning. This type of programmed instructional approach reinforces student knowledge.

For maximum effect on student learning, it is highly recommended that entry activities count significantly toward students' grades, and that corrected start-up assignments be returned within the class period. Research states that quick student feedback (papers returned within one or two days) is critical to student motivation (Bangert-Downs, Kulik, Kulik, & Morgan, 1991; Gilbert, 2010; Hattie & Timperley, 2007; Wees, 2010). Quick feedback allows the student to make the necessary adjustments for improved performance.

Entry Activities Allow for Assessment

Entry activities can also be used as a long-range memory assessment tool. Performance on these assignments provides teachers and paraprofessionals necessary information about individual students' processing and retention ability. Using information gained through this practice, teachers can devise and implement differentiated instruction and innovative approaches to assist struggling students. Even during the entry activity, there is time for students who are struggling to get limited assistance from the teacher. Peer coaching can also be utilized during the entry activity.

Entry Activity and Lesson Example

We have found that having the entry activity visible as the students enter the classroom helps the students get focused on the lesson. Setting students up for success requires an environment that is well managed with the understanding that all materials and lessons are in place prior to the students' arrival. Each minute of the instructional period should be carefully calculated. No wasted time. Wasted time opens the door for disruptions.

A visible display of the day's operations should be available to students for each class period to ensure a smooth start. The following are examples of what could be displayed as the students enter the classroom.

Elementary Entry Activity and Lesson Example

Entry Activity and Lesson
Thursday, August 14
Math (1–3)

** Today's Supplies—(1) Textbook, (2) Folder, (3) Writing Materials

Independent—Entry Activity

1. List numbers 1–50.

2. Circle even numbers.

3. Put a square around each fifth number.

Group—Share answers and discuss with class.

Independent—Complete Section 3 in textbook.

Group—Exchange papers and correct.

Independent—Do problems 1–20 in textbook.

Secondary Entry Activity and Lesson Example

Entry Exercise and Lessons for
Thursday, August 14
Employers expect their employees to be
punctual, prepared, productive, and polite.
Production = 50% of the grade

** Important Notes:

Journal entries will not be accepted after five minutes past the tardy bell. Place the journal entry on the cart when done. [Note to the reader: This prevents students from copying others students' journal entries.]

Get a textbook from the shelf to use for today's assignment.

Reminder: Binder check tomorrow.

US History

Independent—Journal Entry—Who were the Freedmen?

Independent—Finish reading Article Analysis 6.4 in your textbook.

Group—Answer the question to 6.4.

Independent—Read Article Analysis 6.5, and write a one-page expository response.

Helping Students Stay on Task

Finding out what students value is important to the learning process. Students don't always agree with certain rules; however, they do have to follow them. Understanding that certain school rules might conflict with home rules opens the door for teaching students how to be flexible and cooperative in the school setting. This concept adds support for managing the classroom and defiant behaviors. If we know what students value, we can tie it to the lesson and move forward.

Similarly, considering our students' maturity levels will help us create realistic expectations for their time on task in the classroom. Development of the frontal lobes is incomplete until the early twenties. Because this area is responsible for impulse control and planning, its incomplete development may explain much about adolescent behavior (Strauch, 2004).

Anyone who has worked with teenagers knows this to be true. One day a student wants to be a kindergarten teacher; the next day the same student wants to be a cosmetologist. Understanding that teenagers are just as confused about themselves as those who watch the maturing process will help in dealing with what is perceived as defiant behavior.

True Encounter

A high school basketball coach had a point guard who could compete with any other guard in the league until the young man's performance began to drop. Things continued to go downhill and the young man lost his starting position. When the coach spoke with the young man, he discovered the young man's father had lost his job and the family was probably going to move. It was the young man's first year at the school, and he had proven himself as a student and an athlete. This was becoming a common practice since this was his second high school in two years due to family moves. Each time he had to prove himself, and he was getting tired of moving.

The coach went to the whiteboard and began to draw boxes. He asked the young man to tell him areas of interest (friends, sports, hobbies), and duties (family, school, basketball, job). As the young man shared, the coach began to place each item in a box. He asked the young man to tell him what he saw on the board. The young man shared that each item had its own box. It was at that point the coach pointed to the box with basketball written in it and said, "Do you see anything else in this box?" The young man responded, "No." "That's right," the coach said. "However, you have allowed your father's job situation to get into the basketball box, and when that happens, you cannot give your total attention to basketball when you need to. You have no control over what happens with your father's job. You do have total control over what happens with your basketball performance. The team is counting on you. Can you keep your mind on basketball when you need to and family when you need to?" The young man went on to regain his starting position, became a team leader, and high point scorer.

Outside distracters were getting in the way, until the perceptive coach decided to invest in the young man's life beyond basketball. What would happen in the classroom if teachers took interest in their students' personal lives?

Accountability Jar: A Strategy for Helping K–5 Students Manage Their Behavior

This strategy helps younger students manage their on-task behavior. It combines group and individual accountability which lead to self-starters. Placing two jars (one empty and one full of marbles) at the front of the room provides visual and audible reinforcement for acceptable and unacceptable behavior.

When the class is on task or performing at expected levels, marbles are added to the (formerly) empty jar by teacher choice or class decision. The sound of dropping the marble in the jar draws attention, and seeing the marble dropped adds to the positive reward being given. When unacceptable behavior is observed, marbles can be moved back to the original jar, also by teacher choice or group decision.

The key to this technique is making sure the final outcome or reward (to be provided when the formerly empty jar becomes full) is identified by a group decision and is something that the class is willing to corporately work toward. Examples might include a class outing, a party, or special entertainment. We brought in the local NFL team's quarterback one year as a reward for the best-behaved PE class.

Gaining and Keeping Control

W.I.N.—What's Important Now?

Teachers looking to improve their instructional delivery are in a constant state of self-evaluation. There should be no second-guessing, but quality review of where class behavior and instruction are headed.

Teachers must constantly ask themselves, What's important at the given moment in the class? Is it student concerns, a notice from the office, the phone ringing, an e-mail, or the lesson and its components?

This is a particularly important question when things are starting to unravel. Teachers have the right to change rules or procedures when they sense their original expectations are not worth fighting for. One of the greatest frustrations among teachers is the unfulfilled desire to see students consistently on task and thirsty to learn. This is not a realistic expectation. We are dealing with nature's most random creatures, and they often operate in a pack mode. Checking student perception of how things are going in each class period, and being prepared to switch it up at a moment's notice, has the potential to create mutual respect between teacher and students.

Timing Is Everything!

Knowing when to transition is something that comes with experience. Student attention span and ability to absorb new information varies and increases with age. The older the student, the longer the attention span. (In kindergarten, it is 1 to 2 minutes; in 12th grade, it is 10 to 15 minutes.) So attention spans vary from 1 to 15 minutes; when your class's attention starts to wane, it's time to introduce something else.

Research has shown that three shifts in instructional delivery during a 60-minute class are best to keep student focus at its highest point (Middendorf & Kalish, 1996). Your arsenal of delivery methods should include lectures to the whole class, group activities, and the various forms of electronic delivery, including both online content and content your school may own on a server or DVD. Changing delivery methods every 10 to 15 minutes keeps the lesson fresh and engaging. Designing lessons with multiple instructional approaches to reach the same objective is helpful in maintaining class control.

Defiant students will attempt to derail the lesson due to their lack of ability to stay focused on what is being taught, and they try

> ### Remember This
>
> Disruptive behavior almost always precedes defiant behavior. When disruptive behavior surfaces and is dealt with, it would behoove the teacher to expect defiance to follow.
>
> Once disruptive behavior begins, and before teachers intervene, they should ask themselves why the student is acting this way or what might have brought about the behavior. If the teacher feels that the student has no legitimate reason for this behavior and intervention is necessary, it is wise to expect that the disruptive behavior will progress into defiance.

to take as many classmates as they can with them. One mutineer has little effect on the whole and usually is ignored by the group. If it is necessary to deal with defiant students, make sure they do not get the satisfaction of slowing down instruction. It is best to wait until the class is working on an assignment and talk to defiant students one-on-one. If a student has a tendency to be volatile, be prepared to discuss the issue outside the class setting. Perhaps it will be best to meet with such a student during recess, lunch, or planning time.

Regular review of their choices will prepare teachers for a ready and timely response when they must choose how to respond to defiant behavior. Teachers should mentally review a variety of scenarios and evaluate how they could best respond when various situations occur in their classrooms. After evaluating the student's behavior and assessing what sets off the behavior, they must consider what action must be taken to diminish disruptive and defiant behaviors.

Bringing Disruptive Students Back Into the Fold

Wait Time and Silence

One way to end disruption is to stop lesson delivery and be silent. When dialogue stops, disruptive students get nervous and wonder why they are not competing for attention. A brief pause in lesson delivery can help them refocus. It is during wait time that the teacher's allies will begin to emerge, and the self-starters begin to correct and lead fellow classmates. Student leaders will control the class for you and challenge their classmates to cooperate.

Give Them a Job

The defiant and disruptive students often lead the charge of class disruption. Therefore, it is often beneficial to give them a role in the instructional process. Examples might include assisting with worksheet distribution, leading a question-and-answer period, reading aloud to others, or similar classroom activities.

There Is Power in an Individual's Name

An individual's name is one of the most powerful attention-getting diversions. When it is necessary to gain a disruptive student's attention and wait time or silence is not working, addressing students by name is helpful. Asking them a question develops a form of constructive embarrassment that will get their attention and bring the focus back to the lesson.

Enter a Student's Personal Space

Students value their personal space and find it threatening if the teacher enters their space uninvited. When the defiant or disruptive student is acting out, it is often helpful in controlling the behavior to stand near the disruptive student, or slowly pass by the student's desk, or check the student's progress on an assignment. This act will get the student's attention refocused. Many times this type of student desires the attention of the teacher. Providing attention often brings the refocusing needed.

This method has proven to be effective when the teacher does not break the pace of the lesson while invading a disruptive student's area. Bringing the lesson to the disruptive student's station demonstrates a willingness to abandon the delivery post and bring the lesson to where the student is.

Conferencing at the Student's Desk

Personal one-on-one time often brings about the necessary reconnect for teacher and student. This is a good time to review expectations and desires and to clarify needs and wants of teacher and student. As we move toward connecting with difficult students, this type of interaction can bring about desired behavior.

But be careful to pay attention to the student's intentions in asking for the one-on-one meeting. The purpose might be to divert you so others can join in the misbehavior. Don't get trapped into these visits at the desk, and don't let students create guilt because they can't get you to come to their desk whenever they want.

Remember This

There is a fine balancing act between *need* and *want*.

Monitoring the Difficult Class

Sometimes it becomes necessary to abandon direct instruction for monitoring students working on an assignment. This occurs when the class is difficult to manage and instruction is limited due to class unrest. The unrest could be due to a schoolwide trauma, upcoming vacation, return from vacation, or disagreement over classroom procedures. Teaching can become limited if the pack is more interested in attacking and disrupting the learning process.

At these times, focus on management. It might be necessary to engage students with increased rigor. You might need to walk among the desks, looking at what each student is working on, making sure that all students are on task rather than helping students to understand the subject or improve their work. Keep the group focused on the subject and off the disruption. Most classes will miss the interaction and personal attention from the teacher and begin the process of self-adjusting their behavior. Often the students will begin to hold each other accountable.

Another approach is to address the problem directly with the class: Name the issue that you believe is causing the disruption (e.g., upcoming vacation, traumatic incident) and describe how you see the incident affecting class behavior. Give students an opportunity to voice their concerns. We have noticed a positive behavior change and increased production after a sincere interaction with these students.

Managing Conflict

Conflict between students can be a major disruption in class. Here we present two strategies for dealing with this kind of conflict.

Conflict Mediation

We use this process, illustrated in Figure 4.2, at the high school level with trained students leading mediations. These interventions are done without staff involvement. However, staff must be available to assist. This process also works at the middle school level with staff assistance.

The process begins with one student submitting a complaint to an administrator or teacher. The staff person who received the complaint assigns the complaining student to a student mediator chosen from a list of trained students. Then the student mediator solicits agreement from both students involved to participate in the mediation process. The process is effective only with willing participants.

> **Remember This**
>
> A modified impromptu use of this process can work in crisis situations, such as fights, verbal arguments, and threats.

Using this process, we have discovered that students involved in conflict usually have had a misunderstanding, and when the process is complete, they can depart with a mutual agreement for dealing with each other in the future.

Figure 4.2   Conflict Mediation

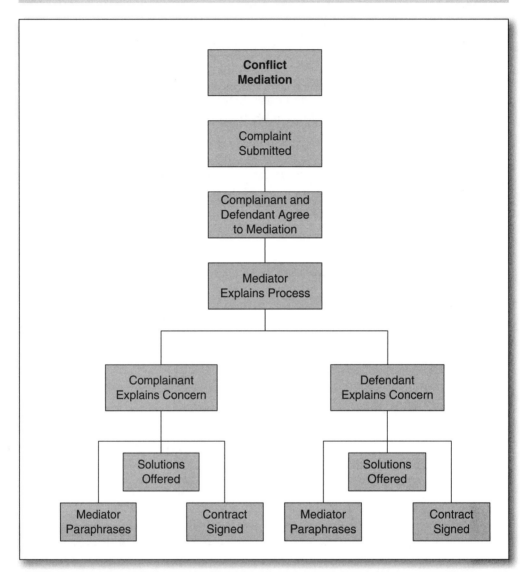

Ground Rules

The mediator explains the following rules to both parties before the process begins:

1. The students in conflict will take turns sharing their concerns with the mediator. The mediator will record all comments.

2. While sharing his concerns, Participant A may look at and speak only to the mediator.

3. Participant B may not speak until it is his turn. If participant B interrupts the reporting of participant A, the mediator will remind participant B only once that he must wait his turn. If participant B continues to interrupt, he will be removed from the room and lose the right to hear the report of participant A.

4. The process will be repeated for participant B.

5. An open discussion will take place once the reporting is complete. The goal of the discussion will be to create ways to address similar problems in the future.

6. At the conclusion of the discussion, participants A and B and the mediator will sign a contract explaining the situation, solutions, and review date.

The Mediation Process

1. The complainant reports first.

2. When the reporting person is finished speaking, the mediator asks the following question: "Is there anything else you would like added to your comments?"

3. After any additional information is recorded, the mediator asks clarifying questions and paraphrases the report for added understanding.

4. The second participant is provided a chance to share her report. She is not allowed to address the other participant's comments.

5. When she is done speaking, the mediator asks the following question again: "Is there anything else you would like added to your comments?"

6. After any additional information is recorded, the mediator asks clarifying questions and paraphrases the report for added understanding.

7. After any both sides have made their reports, and the notes have been clarified, an open discussion takes place regarding how the students will solve similar conflicts in the future. The mediator facilitates this.

8. The mediator drafts a contract (see Figure 4.3) explaining the situation and solutions, and solicits agreement to it from both parties. It includes a date for review of the contract; the review

is a check-in with the two parties for the purpose of confirming that the contract is being followed or identifying that it needs amending. The mediator is responsible for making sure the review takes place on the date set in the contract.

9. The mediator and both participants sign the contract.

Figure 4.3   Conflict Management Resolution and Contract

Complainant(s):

Defendant(s):

Date: _____   Review Date: _____

Issue Notes (from student reports):

Resolutions (How did students resolve this conflict?):

Agreements (How will students resolve future conflicts?):

Evidence Demands a Verdict

Sometimes students will lie to avoid consequences. When you suspect this is the case, you can use this strategy to find out what has happened and to address the underlying issue. The strategy works best after the suspect has been confronted about a situation that arose in a group setting, such as a classroom, an assembly, or a bus. The process provides the necessary evidence to justify your verdict without getting into a power struggle with the suspected student. It is perfect for situations in which you suspect there were inappropriate comments, stealing, assault, or extortion, or where you suspect a student harbored contraband.

To begin, ask the suspect student to tell you what was said or done. If the student refuses to admit error, move to the following process:

1. Isolate all possible witnesses in a group setting so they cannot talk to each other or see each other's responses.

2. Hand out a piece of paper to each student who could have knowledge about the situation you are investigating. Tell them to write down who said or did what. Tell them not to put their names on the papers.

3. Have students place the papers in an isolated spot away from you to ensure confidentiality. You must allow the witnesses total anonymity to get reliable information. Tell students to return to their seats after they submit their papers.

4. When the process is complete and all students have submitted their papers anonymously, review what the students have written. Common responses will lead you to the correct verdict in a fair and equitable way. Now you can intervene with the guilty party in a productive way.

5. Give the suspect another chance to admit the error. A gentle and tactful approach with the suspect will allow you to build your relationship with the student.

6. If the student confesses, your investigation is complete, and the healing process can begin.

7. If the student still will not admit to the error, share the findings from the papers that indicate guilt. Review the information with the student. Ask him why he said or did what he did.

8. Keep working for a confession while explaining that you want to trust the student. Offer the student a choice: If he admits the error now, all will be forgiven. If he continues to resist, it will lead to a parent phone call and an office referral. Tell the student to think about it.

9. Leave the student alone.

10. Come back in a few minutes and ask about the situation again. If an admission is still not forthcoming, make the parent phone call and office referral.

> ### Remember This
>
> We are trying to stir the soul and heal a relationship that has been damaged because the student lied to you. Confession is good for the soul and will help heal the relationship.

Dealing With Interruptions

We all have experienced the following scenarios. When the classroom door opens, all eyes go to the intruder. The teacher must not become alarmed or annoyed when learning has been interrupted. The learning has only shifted to another format until the intruder leaves.

Give attention when attention is due. Otherwise keep on teaching. Grace under fire is a good philosophy. Calm during an interruption brings about calm in the classroom. The following examples offer suggestions for how to deal with various interruptions.

Scenarios for Specific Problems

Office Slips

It is best to make as little of the intrusion as possible. If an office slip needs to be given to a student, check the time to see when it must be responded to. If it is not until later in the period, set it aside as if nothing has happened, and keep the lesson moving. If the student is requested right away, ask her to come to the door, and then give her the slip so she can leave directly without returning to her seat. This keeps the other students from getting involved with why the student is leaving.

Messages from the office regarding students needing to call home or get a ride can be given to the students at the end of class. Inform students receiving messages that they need to get their messages at the end of class; they rarely forget.

> **Remember This**
>
> Youngsters are social creatures. Any information they receive is exciting and must be shared with their peers. Keeping the information from the student until it must be shared will reduce the impact on instructional time.

Phone Calls and Intercom Requests

Do your best to avoid taking phone calls during instructional time. Most phone systems have a message program. Let the voice message pick up the call. Many calls are student related and require time to process outside of student hearing and instructional time. Taking time away from the lesson opens the door to student disruptions, and the classroom environment may become compromised. Students know when the teacher is not in a position to interact with them.

If you must take a call, address the caller professionally without getting into a dialogue about the request. You can discuss the call outside instructional time. Keeping the conversation succinct and to the point gives the students as little information as possible. Instruction can move on if a controversy over the call is not allowed.

> **Remember This**
>
> Youngsters enjoy controversy, as insignificant as it might be. Being aware of student interest in controversies is vital in controlling the learning environment.

Fires, Lockdowns, and Earthquakes

Each of these requires grace under fire. Prior planning and careful thought must be given to each of these situations. Most schools have specific procedures and roles for faculty members in the event of a building-wide emergency.

Make sure to convey these plans to the students at the beginning of the school year. Students are generally compliant during a crisis and look to the teacher for clear thinking and calm leadership. We have found that the most defiant students will cooperate when they think they are in a dangerous situation. Sometimes they take a leadership role in such cases.

Snow

In climates where snow is a rare event, it can bring about an added distraction to the instructional process. If possible, close the window shades and keep the lesson moving.

Flying and Crawling Insects

Keeping screens on windows is a big help in keeping out insects, but insects will intrude on occasion. We have found that a valuable lesson can be taught when these intruders arrive. Switch up the lesson plan for the moment. The designed lesson is not going to take place until you have dealt with the interruption. Instead, require all students to remain seated, as they too will want to fly around the room. Some will try to kill the critter, while others will want to save it. If possible, capture the intruder and return it to the outside. The hunters in the room will be upset, but they will get over it much faster than any budding entomologists in the room, who will want to study the insect.

In the event the insect is a bee, it must be explained to the students that for the safety of those deathly allergic to beestings, the bee must be done away with. This can create a teachable moment regarding allergies and concern for classmates.

Remember This
We have witnessed huge emotional withdrawals and shutdowns in students when they are begging for mercy for the insect and the teacher kills it or approves of its death.

Students Returning From the Office

Students returning to the classroom often create a disruption, as the other students want to know what happened. Debriefing students returning from the office is vital to stabilizing the classroom atmosphere. Intercepting the student at the door will allow for the necessary exchange of expectations for both the teacher and the student. Behavior expectations need to be clarified before reentry is allowed.

Remember This

Meet with administration prior to the beginning of the school year and establish expectations for the instructional environment. An example might be that students should not return to the room during class time due to the disruption reentry causes.

Remember This

Students thrive on new information. It is a good idea to establish the expectation that a student returning to the class does not enter without talking with the teacher first.

The Power of Red

The use of a red screen on PowerPoint or overhead projectors can serve as a signal that all mouths should stop, or consequences will follow. For the overhead projector, a red transparency can be made with a page protector with red cellophane inserted. The red transparency allows the text to be seen on the screen, yet sends the message that it is time to get focused.

Youngsters see everything.

When the screen goes red, heads turn, and learning becomes focused.

Note: Use intermittently for full effect. Simply picking up the red transparency and holding it where students can see it also sends the message that it could be used if the students fail to manage themselves.

Addressing Open Challenges

Calculated action must be taken when open defiance takes place. When a defiant student makes an open challenge to authority, the student is asking the question, Who's in charge? Open challenges may be overt or covert. Covert challenges could include irritant noise such as tapping a pencil, clicking a pen, crinkling paper, or repeated sniffing. These behaviors appear to be normal, yet the student is begging for the teacher to react, which would open the door for the defiant student to attack. Much caution must be taken when addressing these behaviors. It is best to speak with these students privately, and do not let them know, in the class setting, what you want to talk with them about. Wait until you have them in the hall or the back of the class. Choose the setting carefully, for the defiant student will seek to exploit the situation.

Gang members are known for their attempts to intimidate staff and students. Gang members must prove themselves to the gang through this type of behavior. Knowing what their motive is will be helpful when the moment arrives. The more knowledge teachers have regarding gangs and gang behavior in the school and community, the more effective they will be in dealing with these defiant students.

Overt attempts to take control of the instructional setting are easiest to address, because there is no question about where or whom they are coming from. The only remaining question a teacher needs to answer prior to action is, Why is the student acting out? This question needs to be considered, and a careful and calculated approach needs to be thought out before action is taken (see pp. 3–4). Not every scenario can be anticipated; however, teachers should take the time to preplan their responses.

We have found that covert or mutinous behavior is the most difficult to address, due to its behind-the-scenes or underground approach. We have intercepted plans to sabotage another teacher's lessons by pushing the teacher's hot buttons, which gets them upset, or by engaging the teacher in an off-topic discussion. Students who know what gets a teacher off track will take advantage of that knowledge.

Knowing what your weaknesses are will enable you to deal with the challenges that will come. This will also prepare you for addressing the issues while keeping instruction moving forward. Don't let pride get in the way of countering a challenge. Work through the process with the leader one-on-one outside the instructional setting.

Anticipation and Foresight

Being realistic, understanding, and well read about student behavior is necessary for proper engagement, relationship building, and teaching. We are not always able to anticipate what will happen in a given situation; therefore, experience must be the teacher. Educators new to the field of education will do themselves a great service by talking to more experienced members of the staff, and asking them how they handle certain behaviors and situations. No teacher can afford to be an island. Anticipating what a student will do to intentionally or unintentionally derail the lesson prepares teachers so they can adjust the lesson to avoid the inevitable disruptions.

> **Remember This**
>
> Showing offense at the disruption gives the student power, knowledge of the teacher's weaknesses, and a stick with which to beat the teacher.

Maintain Self-Control

When a disruption does occur, deal with it professionally and move on. Maintaining self-control is a necessary skill for the teacher. There are times when your natural tendency may be to become angry

> **Remember This**
>
> Keep pushing forward until there is a lull. Don't take instructional time to work through unruly behavior. You always have time to formally address a defiant student later.

and aggressive. This is the signal to stop and reassess what is causing the internal conflict you are feeling. Remember, nobody can make you angry unless you give your permission.

As adults we have learned how to control our anger and frustrations. If we are going to teach our students to do the same, we must first be willing to demonstrate the proper response. The best way to avoid being taken over by anger is to ask the question we have touched on before: What is causing the behavior we are concerned with? When we begin to understand the situation, we will be less likely to react to it.

De-escalating Student Anger

Not always can we find the soft and thoughtful method for dealing with defiant and disruptive behaviors. There are times when it is

> **Remember This**
>
> Dangerous situations must be dealt with immediately.

necessary to take aggressive and calculated action. Critical situations need to be handled without student input. The teacher may need to take action to avoid injury to self or others. The last resort is to place hands on a student; however, there are times when physical restraint is necessary.

There is a time for controlled assertiveness by the teacher, through a raised voice and limited physical contact, to avoid student or teacher injury. Calm and calculated intervention steps are paramount in these situations. Rapidly identifying the source of the conflict is

> **Remember This**
>
> Adrenalin and hormones often block outside reception to the point where the combatant will not be able to listen; however, they are capable of hearing. Hence, an interruption such as loud voice, whistle, unfamiliar sound, or first name will get their attention.

imperative, and calculated assessment of the situation is vital to avoid escalation. Before engaging in a conflict, it is necessary to identify the combatants and the issues in question. Calling on the combatants by first name gets their attention. We have found that when a new voice or sound enters the conflict, attention is momentarily diverted away from the combatants. It is during these moments that de-escalation begins.

Isolating the combatants is necessary until rational thought is obtained. Any physical engagement with students should be avoided, and is necessary only when individuals are being hurt. If physical contact is needed, we have found that identifying and subduing the most aggressive combatant usually brings a halt to the conflict. Once the combatant is subdued and under the control of a staff member, a gentle word reassuring the student that everything is okay, and that the physical con-

Remember This

Conflict mediation will work only with willing participants.

flict is over, will gently bring the student's thoughts and actions back to a functional point. Separation is still necessary between combatants. The combatants should be taken to a quiet place for counseling, conflict mediation (see pp. 77–80), or police intervention.

True Encounter

Over the security radio system came notification that a fight was taking place in the student commons. By the time administrators, deans of students, and security personnel arrived, a crowd of several hundred students had gathered. Two students were engaged in an all-out fight. The assistant principal had to physically force his way through the crowd of students.

Once the assistant principal got to the fighters, he approached the most aggressive student and placed a half nelson around the student's head and arm. Putting his head next to the student's ear, he stated in an assertive voice, "This is the assistant principal. You need to stop." The student did stop, the situation deescalated, and the area returned to calm.

The combative students were then taken to the office, where mediation and problem solving took place.

Mutiny

Remember This

Teachers are only as effective as the support they have from administration.

We have found that mutiny is often teacher imposed. It's a strong signal from the students that a misunderstanding has taken place and that unrealistic teaching methods are being implemented. Students are fairly flexible and understanding; however, they are very sensitive to unjust treatment. They talk about what they perceive to be right in the world, and are often very vocal when things are not going as they believe they should.

The persistence of unfair treatment or failure to address unrest and complaints will lead to diminished instructional time and a power struggle. Power struggles are a no-win situation, and instructional time will be lost.

Negotiate

We have found that the best way to regain control is to engage in an open discussion with the students using the conflict mediation process (see pp. 77–80). The teacher must remain the leader of the class and serves as mediator. Students may share concerns using the conflict mediation process. The teacher should paraphrase for clarity and guide the discussion. Concerns should be recorded where all can see them to increase the validity of the process. Follow-up is essential; the process must include setting a follow-up date to ensure that all parties' needs are being met.

Being humble is important. Letting the students know that classroom issues will be addressed demonstrates care and interest in students' concerns about classroom procedures. Open dialogue creates trust between students and teacher. Students can make a difference in the classroom and should have a say in how the class operates.

Open negotiation is healthy and can bring about a mutual understanding about how the class should operate. If students have input into the class process, there are greater odds of class buy-in. Compromise and negotiations provide the students with a real sense of empowerment. When teacher and students work together at compromising and negotiating rules, assignments, curriculum, and instruction, mutiny will become a foreign concern of the teacher, as the students work toward the common good of the class.

> **Remember This**
>
> The classroom should be about unity in purpose with the teacher acting as guide.

Buy Time With an Assignment

The tactics used for bringing disruptive students back into the fold (see p. 75) can also be effective in quelling a mutiny. For example, as soon as the defiant behavior begins to disrupt and derail instruction, give the class a brief impromptu assignment that reinforces what is being taught. Give the assignment while standing next to the most defiant student. While the class is working on the assignment, you can address the defiant student's behavior and head off the mutiny.

A good interception question when disruptions begin to surface is, "Did you have something to say?" Be ready for an inappropriate response. Turn the table by tying the defiant response to the lesson. This approach gets the disrupter and the class refocused without embarrassing anyone.

Address Pack Behavior

Disruptive students operate like wolves in the wild. This type of student often looks for a teacher's faults in the form of misspelled words in class materials, perceived unfair rules, too much homework, wrong usage of words in speaking to the class, wrong grades assigned, mistakes in taking attendance, or untimely notices. These types of issues are somewhat petty. However, the defiant student will look to attack in order to gain attention or disrupt the learning process.

Assign Seating

Keep the pack separated. They only have strength in numbers. We have found that when a pack member is isolated from the others, he is not nearly as aggressive. One-on-one encounters usually lead to the student backing down, and signs of compliance begin (see pp. 65–66).

Redirect Challenges and Diversions to Out-of-Class Time

Wolves like to create a diversion while they are setting up for an attack. When a disruptive student begins to ask off-topic questions, it is prudent to first assess if the question has anything to do with the topic. Ask the student (in a sincere and gentle way), What does your question have to do with the subject? If the answer has nothing to do with the subject (it's usually a personal issue designed for attention getting), inform the questioning student that an answer can be discussed during noninstructional time.

> **Remember This**
>
> Keep the door open for dialogue.

Going against our natural desire to take on disruptive behavior through arguing, sarcasm, or angry retaliatory comments is one of the hardest lessons to learn. Simply directing the attacking student to address complaints with you before school, at recess or lunch, or after school keeps the door open for the disgruntled student and allows the class to keep pursuing the lesson.

Working With Administration

Three Good Reasons to Involve Administration

1. When all other interventions have been tried. Administration is the teacher's ace.

2. When there is a missing student who cannot be accounted for.

3. When a student has become violent or persists in disrupting the learning process.

Administrators are the support system for the classroom; they are not the managers of the classroom. They make use of clearly established processes recorded in handbooks, district and building policies, classroom rules, and state laws to support teachers.

When it is necessary to send a student to the office, all classroom options should have been utilized. Administrators who know the teacher has exhausted all classroom options will be much more willing to deal effectively, efficiently, and quickly with the student on behalf of the teacher. After such a referral, the relationship with the administration needs to be strengthened by a follow-up visit from the sending teacher. We have assisted several teachers who felt they had little or no support from administration, and visits such as this one will keep the communications open and the relationship healthy.

Sometimes administration is overwhelmed with their responsibilities. Providing them with information about how you will be managing your class can encourage them. Administrators appreciate teachers' attempts to maintain a high level of classroom control and solve problems in the classroom, avoiding unnecessary administration involvement.

Most states have laws about student discipline and the penalties that can be imposed if a student wants to disrupt the learning of others. Education is a constitutional mandate to the states, and to not offer education can be considered an act of treason. The failure to educate the young puts a nation at risk of not being able to compete on the global market. If students attempt to disrupt the learning of others, they are in violation of state and federal law. From this perspective, it is important to know when to involve probation officers or police in student discipline.

Remember This

Some states can impose a misdemeanor charge, fine, or detention for disrupting the educational process. Students do not know this, and learning about it does get them back on track. Use this information in select situations and only after administration has been informed.

If Something Can Go Wrong, It Will

Your Back-Up Plan

Always have a back-up plan; the defiant and disruptive students do.

Students are masters at finding the loophole, even when you think you have all the angles covered. There is something about how youngsters are wired that gives them the edge. It's a good idea to explore new ideas with trusted students to get their thoughts on how your proposed plan will work and where the problems are.

Even with such preparation, be prepared with a back-up plan each time you incorporate an intervention. This book is full of fall-back plans that can help teachers get control of disruptive behavior as soon as it starts. Having a back-up plan is vital when things start to unravel.

Leave no stone unturned. You never know what's under the next rock. Continue to develop new strategies and modify ones that are working for you. One approach does not work for every situation. Be prepared to change up your intervention at a moment's notice.

Know Your Students

In chemistry, it is helpful to know what can be a catalyst. The same is true in the classroom. Certain students can ignite the class on a moment's notice. Knowing the individuals or situations that trigger disruptions can also lead to preventive measures.

Getting to know your students individually will solve many of your concerns. Students who know you have a genuine interest in them will generally comply with a reasonable request, because they also know a bit more about you. Knowing your students' tendencies under various situations will help prevent things from going wrong.

Making Wholesale Changes in Classroom Operations

When things are going wrong, it may be useful to introduce new expectations or class procedures. It is best to build into the daily plan a time when open discussion of the change can take place, and to inform the students of the upcoming change. A day's notice is sufficient.

Example of a Needed Change

Unfulfilled expectation: All students need to have something to write with *before they come to class.*

Questions to ask yourself when considering amendment: What are the consequences, to both individual students and the class as a whole, if students don't have something to write with?

- How much time is going to be lost while a student disrupts other students asking for something to write with?
- How many students will be taken advantage of or be strong-armed for a writing tool?
- Is this expectation really worth enforcing?

Amended expectation: Everyone needs to have something to write with *before the tardy bell rings.* Asking another student for something to write with is the same thing as not being prepared. If you need something to write with, the teacher will provide it, and your points for the 4 P's will be reduced (see Chapter 2).

This amended expectation gives students more ownership and reduces class disruptions and student conflict.

Teachers should be constantly reviewing their class procedures by asking themselves the following question: Are the procedures meeting my needs and those of the students? Often teachers create their own monsters. Be willing to switch it up.

Class Closure

The students anticipated the ringing of the bell as I informed them of what was going to take place the next day. As the bell rang and students made their way to the door, I shouted, "See you tomorrow!" Several students were given a personal send-off regarding class expectations or congratulations on an assignment or test as they departed. A few students returned the gesture with "Good-bye" or "Have a nice day, Mr. Korb."

The bell rang for the final time as the week came to an end. As students headed off to who knows where, I shouted, "Remember—Be safe and don't do what Mr. Korb wouldn't do!" Several responded, "Yeah right! That sounds boring." Others couldn't wait to get out the door. The few stragglers told me to be safe on my motorcycle ride home.

The end of the day is a good time to connect with defiant and disruptive students on a positive note if they demonstrated acceptable behavior. Tell them you appreciated their behavior. Be specific about something they did. It's also a good time to remind them about assignments or projects coming due.

Successful classroom management is perhaps the greatest motivator for students wanting to return to the classroom each day. I believe it's because they know we care about them and what they do.

Always have the students put their chairs away and clean up their area. This establishes an atmosphere of professionalism. Then, when the Daily Performance Sheets have been scored and materials put away, it is helpful to send the class off with a clear note of direction for the next class session. This provides security and establishes leadership on the teacher's part. Students appreciate knowing what lies ahead.

A sincere send-off at the end of the class is important for maintaining relationships. A handshake with a genuine parting comment at the door is a great way to demonstrate caring support for each student.

Summary: Common Classroom Scenarios—Guiding Parameters and Corrective Interventions

The common scenarios listed below provide sequential steps of intervention that should be followed in the order given. As a point of clarity, when the term *time-out* is mentioned, the reference is to the refocus station. When the word *removal* is used, the reference is to the hallway. Additionally, the CBIP should be incorporated with any method of disciplinary intervention in or out of the classroom.

Violent Outbursts

Guiding Parameters:

- Intercept behavior at the door.
- Control inflammatory situations.
- Know what sets off the behavior.

Remember This

Do not let the disgruntled student leave the classroom or the building without dealing with the issue, and reassuring the student that the concern will be addressed fairly.

Remember This

The custodial staff will be grateful for the effort to keep the room clean. It will make their job easier, allowing them more time to attend to other needs. When your room is kept clean, it's amazing how fast your requests for classroom needs are met. Emotional banking works for all of us and helps build the relationship with colleagues.

Remember This

Not every student should be or wants to be touched. Others want to be touched too much. Therefore, a brief pat on the shoulder or handshake sends the proper message of "I care about you."

- Negotiate seat assignment.
- Negotiate options (self-removal, one-on-one time).

Corrective Interventions:

1. Review agreements
2. Provide options
3. Removal from the room
4. Call office

Defiant

Guiding Parameters:

- Clarify values regarding goals, relationships, and work ethic.
- Negotiate choices and consequences, self-removal.

Corrective Interventions:

1. Time-out and CBIP
2. Removal
3. Call office

Disruptive

Guiding Parameters:

- Clarify values regarding impact on others.
- Discuss relationships with and perception of others.
- Negotiate choices and consequences.

Corrective Interventions:

1. Card behavior
2. Removal and CBIP
3. Call office

Challenger

Guiding Parameters:

- Review Student Learning Survey (see Chapter 2).
- Create diplomatic alternatives.
- Develop options for confrontation before school, at lunch, at recess, or after school.

Corrective Interventions:

1. Review agreements

2. Time-out and CBIP

3. Removal and CBIP for readmittance

Runner

Guiding Parameters:

- Assign seat diagonally opposite the door.
- Discuss the need to run with the student.
- Ask the student where she will go if she runs.
- If the student runs, readmit her to class if she returns.

Corrective Interventions:

1. Intercept at the door

2. Movable clothes rack as barrier

3. Notify office if student leaves and cannot be accounted for

Trash Mouth

Guiding Parameters:

- Explore alternatives.
- Review Student Learning Survey.

Corrective Interventions:

1. Card behavior

2. Removal and CBIP

Rude and Angry

Guiding Parameters:

- Intercept at the door.
- Promote student's academic progress or performance publicly.
- Kill student with kindness.
- Don't take personally.

Corrective Interventions:

1. Review Student Learning Survey

2. One-on-one interview about needs and concerns

3. Time-out and CBIP

4. Removal

Thrower

Guiding Parameters:

- Negotiate rewards and consequences.
- Install a wastebasket hoop.
- Assign seat near wastebasket.

Corrective Interventions:

1. Review agreements

2. Card behavior

3. CBIP at seat

4. Removal

Crying (K–12)

Guiding Parameters:

- Establish parameters—when, where, and why to cry.
- Understand what brings on crying.
- Develop alternatives to crying. (Writing is a good one.)

Corrective Interventions:

1. Review expectations

2. Implement alternatives

3. Self-removal or counselor's office

4. Removal

Touching

Guiding Parameters:

- Establish parameters—when, where, and why touching is okay.
- Develop alternatives. (For example, squeezing Koosh ball, Velcro under desk. Young students needing to touch can alleviate the

need by clawing at the Velcro as a cat uses a scratching post. This has proven to satisfy the need for touching others.)

- Negotiate rewards and discipline.
- Understand why touching is important.

Corrective Interventions:

1. Refocus station

2. Time-out and CBIP

3. Removal

Noncompliant

Guiding Parameters:

- Negotiate performance contract.
- Adjust assignments and scoring criteria.
- Review Student Learning Survey.
- Assign seat.

Corrective Interventions:

1. Performance contract review

2. Preferential seating

3. Time-out and CBIP

4. Assignments and grading criteria readjustment

5. Incentives

Shut Down and Sleeping

Guiding Parameters:

- Seek to understand.
- Negotiate rewards and discipline.
- Define cause and effect.

Corrective Interventions:

1. Student stands in the back of the room, no leaning

2. Reminder of agreements

3. Incentive for any amount of effort

4. Time-out and CBIP

Process and Apply

1. Design a seating arrangement to meet your needs. Include the following:

   Where will you place defiant and disruptive students?

   When will you develop seat assignments?

   How often will you adjust seat assignments?

2. Outline an entry strategy that will work with your particular class and grade level.

3. Explain your plan for getting the students engaged in classwork before the tardy bell.

4. How can intercepting defiant behavior be a good strategy for containing disruptive behavior before it has a chance to get started?

5. Provide two reasons why identifying disruptive behavior at the door establishes a teacher-controlled learning environment.

6. List three strategies you would use for gaining and keeping control of the classroom. Explain how those strategies assist in classroom management.

7. List the pros and cons of behavior strategies used in dealing with the wolf pack.

8. Outline behavioral strategies for dealing with a wolf pack that will work with your particular class and grade level.

9. Outline what you will do tomorrow regarding class openers, operations/interventions, and send-off.

5

Academic Motivation

When the administration at my school decided that history would no longer be taught to special education students in the resource room, all capable students with individualized education programs (IEPs) were moved into regular history classes. At the time, I was a resource room teacher, so the administration felt it would be a good idea for me to teach regular education history and place the resource room students in my classes. Sounded like a good idea. The only problem was, I had been using accommodations for the special needs population and had lost touch with the regular classroom processes.

Many of the students in the regular classes were advanced learners, and they took offense at the teaching strategies geared more for the resource room. It got to the point of mutiny. Academic motivation began to fall off for the regular students; hence, new approaches were necessary to keep their academic motivation high.

Caesar was a student leader. He suggested that the entry quiz include an additional question for regular education students, and that if it were answered correctly, it would replace one of the other questions that was answered incorrectly. I went one better and suggested that if students got all the answers correct, they would receive extra credit. The class liked Caesar's idea, and the fact that I listened to Caesar strengthened the suggestion, so I implemented it. As a result, the regular education students were much more willing to apply themselves.

T he next steps in our journey to successful student management will provide you with strategies to encourage high-functioning students to improve their academic achievement.

Creating an Environment That Motivates Students

Students bring their baggage to school, and the school should be safer than their houses. School should be a place where students can take risks and explore learning without reprisal from classmates or staff. When students believe in the safety of the school setting (academic and physical), they will flourish and excel.

Remove the guessing and reduce lost instruction time by knowing as much as you can about your students' attitudes, energy levels, and emotions before they come into the classroom. Knowing what they are bringing to the class will dictate what lesson delivery will look like— direct, step by step, class interaction, and/or inquiry. Adjusting delivery to student needs demonstrates genuine care for each student.

Develop a Work Ethic

A work ethic is not natural for most students and needs to be encouraged. Today's employers are looking for self-starters who are on time, come prepared to work, have a work ethic, and get along with others. The four P's (see Chapter 3) provide a framework for teaching this ethic.

Student to Life Plans are being added to state high school graduation requirements around the nation, so the duty falls on educational institutions to enforce these precepts as early as kindergarten. As we suggested in Chapter 3, grading should take into account students' work ethic and performance on the four P's as well as their scores on assignments, tests, quizzes, and projects.

Pace the Workload and Establish the Standard

Not every student is capable of the same workload; therefore, establishing assignment deadlines that everyone can achieve is vital. For consistency, it is recommended that a set day of the week be established as the day when assignments are due. A "Monday or Friday" option works well. Defiant students need structure in order to be consistent and held accountable. This is part of standard setting, which enables all students to pace themselves during the workweek. Knowing the standard is crucial in keeping the class running smoothly.

Welcome Their Questions

Student questions come in all forms and for all reasons. It is important to search out the *why* in their questions. Each question calls for an answer. When the defiant student asks a question, teachers often don't answer because of who is asking. Instead, they need to ask themselves, What is the motivation behind the question? The teacher cannot assume the question is designed to derail the class. There could be an academic link to the inquiry.

Teach Them About Resources

Resources, such as books, libraries, and the Internet, empower students. Students armed with knowledge about how to find and use resources will have valuable tools to use in the global community. These same students will also contribute to the development of additional resources as their natural curiosity drives them forward. Likewise, teachers need to keep current on resource shifts and development in order to address student needs.

Grade With Growth in Mind

Green is the color of growth. All students are developing skills and improving at various rates. To mark student errors, green should be used to demonstrate that growth is occurring. In addition, crossing out what students have written should be avoided. Instead, circling errors indicates an area of concern, and a question mark is a sign that the teacher believes the student is on the right track, yet further clarity needs to be provided. Students have indicated that they find green much more acceptable than red.

Remember This

There are varying degrees of accomplishment, and not everyone will be doing the same amount of work within the given timeline. However, if the workload is adjusted for special situations, then the due date for the class should not be compromised.

Establishing the standard early will divert class dissension and mutiny.

Remember This

One of the first tasks in motivating students to learn is to arouse their curiosity and sustain the interest through time. (Helen Keller)

Remember This

Infants and young children appear to be propelled by curiosity, driven by an intense need to explore, interact with, and make sense of their environment. (Lumsden, 1994, para. 1)

Align Teaching With Learning Styles

One of the biggest causes of class problems is when the teaching style and learning styles don't align. The surveys in Chapter 1 will help teachers identify their students' different learning styles. Teachers trained in learning styles can adjust instruction and delivery approach to better match student learning needs. Creating this match greatly reduces the number of disruptions.

Activity Learning

Most students are kinesthetic learners, and students enjoy working with other students. Any time the teacher can create a situation where students create projects or work on an assignment with other students is a win for the teacher and the students. Even the most disruptive students find it easier to stay focused and engaged when they are allowed some freedom to work with others.

Adjust to Attitude Shifts

As teachers design lessons and prepare materials, the one thing they can count on is that something will alter their plans. A teacher must be prepared to adjust the lesson plan on a moment's notice and without hesitation.

When students' attitudes shift, adjust to where they are, and keep teaching. Working with young people is a never-ending journey. As fast as they can think of something, they will move in that direction. Much like chickens with a raccoon in the pen, youngsters run in all kinds of mental and emotional directions. When the individual or class shifts, the teacher needs to figure out how to get to the front of the pack. The speed and direction of the pack are determined by the speed and direction of the leader, and the teacher cannot afford to be back in the pack. The teacher must be the leader.

Be Attuned to Student Understanding

The teacher must be prepared to change the direction of the class when the group begins to get lost or confused. It might be necessary to backtrack and reteach before the lesson moves forward again. It is not constructive to keep pushing forward with new curriculum if the students have not mastered prior steps.

Sometimes the teacher will feel obligated to stay with the lesson plan when things are not going well. The students might be agitated or apathetic, or the lesson could be below or above their ability levels.

When the class is sending a message that the lesson is off target, it is time to change the direction the lesson is going. What works during times likes these is remembering that students do not know all the components of the lesson, and they won't even know if the teacher changes it. Therefore, the teacher has the discretion to modify the lesson when it is necessary.

> ### Remember This
>
> The students don't know when a lesson was changed because they didn't create it. Don't feel obligated to keep pushing through the lesson.

Be Attuned to Student Behavior

Not every lesson is magic. Often things don't go as planned. Recall from Chapter 4 that change in instructional delivery should take place three times in a 50- to 60-minute session. Moving among lectures, slide presentations, group activities, and independent work keeps the lesson fresh and interesting, and changing modes can be a way to address restless behavior. Always be prepared to change the delivery method. If students make a suggestion regarding the method of delivery, find a way to make the change on the spot. Not only will the students feel empowered, disruptive behavior will diminish.

Using Grades to Motivate High-Functioning Defiant and Disruptive Students

Two Motivators That Work

1. Give students an avenue to obtain what they want—a passing grade or higher.

2. Give students control of their grade—a path for students to soar as high as they can through supplemental extra learning.

When high-functioning students are not feeling challenged, the rigor of instruction needs to be increased. Unchallenged students can lead to unrest and disruptions. This is when it becomes necessary to keep these students focused on academics and the learning rigor high.

Score on a Curve

Scoring on the curve lets high performers set the standard. It is an effective way of getting the attention of high-functioning defiant and disruptive students. When they need to be refocused on what's important, the curve gets their attention in a hurry.

When grades and performance are important to students, grading on the curve raises their level of expectation. Comparing themselves with other students is important to this type of student. When they see students of lesser ability outperforming them, they soon begin to get serious and focused on academic performance.

The goal is to get them out of the defiant mode and to become compliant with class expectations and standards.

Use the Entry Activity

The entry activity has a variety of advantages (see Chapter 4), one of which is that it gets students focused on academics as soon as they walk in the door. When this activity is timed (5 to 10 minutes), collected, scored, and returned during the period, the rapid feedback sets the expectation that learning is paramount. It is recommended that performance on the entry activity count toward a significant percentage of the overall grade—we suggest 20%. Asking for a show of hands for high scores also reinforces the value of this activity.

> **Remember This**
>
> The higher the standard, the higher the performance.

Use the Daily Performance Sheet

At the end of the class period, remind students that they need to fill out their Daily Performance Sheets (DPS; see Chapter 3). It is suggested that all materials be put away with the sheet being the only thing left on their desk. Students are then able to focus on their own performance. As the students record their performance, it is important to inform them that they will be turning in their DPS at the end of class.

When students with high expectations of themselves and others are challenged, they will rise to the challenge set before them. High-functioning students often have an overinflated view of their abilities; therefore, they believe they set the standards. If disruptive or defiant behavior has removed the focus from their academic performance, it often is helpful to get the student to do some self-reflecting using the DPS. This gets their focus off being disruptive and defiant and back onto their academic goals.

Set a Weighting Scale

One of the biggest motivators is to let the students have input into the weighting process. Weighting the grade is a helpful tool for placing emphasis on areas of performance the teacher feels are necessary for academic growth. Giving added weight to work related to state academic standards is useful if you are looking for students to meet such standards. Behavior standards are equally valid; for these standards, greater weight might be given to the DPS. For a special needs student, 100% of the grade can be based on the DPS. In a general education class, the DPS might be weighted to count for 50% to 60% of the grade, with assignments, projects, and assessments accounting for the rest.

Provide Opportunities to Adjust Scores

Student control is rated as the highest motivator for student learning. This strategy has been a strong motivator for students of all ages and abilities. When a student is not a good test taker, yet shows high proficiency in production work, opportunities to earn extra credit can be used to counterbalance test scores and bolster the student's grade.

Teachers do not assess students on all the information covered in a unit of study. Testing students on a sampling of the covered material is often sufficient to determine if they have grasped basic concepts. But students do retain additional information that is not assessed. Hence, the following suggestion is offered as a way to provide students an avenue to demonstrate their further understanding of concepts pertinent to the unit of study:

> Assessment scores of 65% or better can be improved upon when the student provides additional accurate information about the subject. Additional information should be written on the test sheet; this prevents students from writing a sheet of information beforehand and turning it in with the assessment. The additional information can be awarded double point value. For example, if the missed question has a value of 5 points, and the student provides additional accurate information about the same topic, the student would be awarded 10 points. The extra points are added to the student's score, which in turn raises the overall score for the assessment.

In our classes, this strategy has yielded greater student efforts to obtain high scores on assessments. The coupling of additional pertinent information has improved overall student performance.

Will Work for Food

Fast food coupons are great incentives for students who go above and beyond expectations, answer tough questions, contribute clarifying information, score 100%, or catch grammatical errors (yours, or errors in the text). This is a great way to build camaraderie between students and teachers. In the corporate world, employees are rewarded for a job well done; this process prepares students for that practice and encourages them to strive for rewards outside those in the typical grading process. Students enjoy the interaction and rise to higher levels of performance when something other than grades is offered for exceptional performance.

Addressing Problems With Academic Performance

Notes From Parents

Assignments turned in after the due date must be accompanied by a note from the student's parents. This creates parent awareness and takes away sticks defiant students beat teachers with. Accountability is the focus when requiring students to bring a note *to the teacher* upon their return from an absence. The high-functioning defiant student will challenge the teacher to check with the attendance office. Students need to be reminded that the classroom is not about attendance taking. The classroom focus is on academics. Require the student to bring a copy of the note to class or get a separate note. The purpose is to keep the parent involved with the student's education. This strategy also forces the students to take responsibility for their own education.

Homework Saver

The intent of the Homework Saver is to provide greater student control of academics and behavior. There will come times when students miss class. To maintain academic motivation, there needs to be a redemption component built into the grading system. The Homework Saver is such a component: It allows a student to skip handing in a homework assignment. The teacher may offer Homework Savers to all students who are caught up on all assignments and tests and who have had no tardies. How many Homework Savers the teacher offers in a grading period will depend upon teacher preference; six is the recommendation.

The intent of the Homework Saver is to encourage students to be managers of their grades. Allowing students to take control of their grades motivates them and provides a way for them to deal with unexpected absences from school. The Homework Saver is an optional device all students can take advantage of to prevent a negative impact on their grade or to rescue themselves from becoming overwhelmed with additional homework after they have been absent.

The Homework Saver also provides an option for students who have discipline issues. Student personal time is important; hence, allowing a student to use one of her Homework Savers in lieu of a detention can be an option. Students can use a form like that in the box below to keep track of their Homework Savers.

Homework Saver

Conditions:

All assignments and tests are completed.

Only six Homework Savers may be used in a semester.

Homework Savers can be forfeited for misbehavior and attendance concerns.

___	___	___	___	___	___
1	2	3	4	5	6

The numbers above represent the allotted number of Homework Savers provided to each student. Teachers can put an X or check on the line above a numeral each time a Homework Saver is used.

Academic Performance Contracts

Sometimes students can be motivated to complete their academic work by being promised they will receive credit if they comply with the steps outlined in a contract. A contract for such a purpose might look like this:

Remember This

Students in control of their learning will excel.

You will receive a passing grade if you complete the following:

- Attend class regularly (only two unexcused absences for the term)
- Turn in all homework assignments
- Take all quizzes and tests
- Correct all incorrect answers on homework, quizzes, and tests during class time

Extreme Absenteeism

Parent phone calls should be made any time a student is absent. It is recommended that when a student reaches the fifth and eighth absences, parents should be notified in writing. The notification should explain the attendance policy and the appeal process, outlined below.

Credit Appeal Hearings

For students who have reached the maximum number of absences allowed before they lose credit for a class, a credit appeal hearing may serve as a last-ditch attempt to retrieve their academic credit. An appeal board should be put together to hear the student's appeal; board members should include the school nurse, a school counselor, school administrators, attendance personnel, a teacher, and a special education teacher (when special education students are involved).

It should be the students' responsibility to arrange for the appeal—they got themselves into the situation, and they should get themselves out. This means they should contact administration and arrange for a time when all can meet. During the hearing, the student provides an argument as to why she should receive her credit. A time limit should be set for this presentation. Once the student presentation is concluded, the appeals board may ask clarifying questions. The appealing student must be informed as to when she will be notified of the appeal board's decision. It is recommended that the decision be delivered after a brief recess of the board.

The appeal board can (1) deny the credit and require the student to attend in-school suspension for the rest of the semester during the class period or periods for which credit was denied, or (2) write a contract outlining the expectation for retrieving the credit.

Note: Students who choose not to appeal should be placed in in-school suspension during the period when the class is conducted for which they will receive no credit. The goal is to provide an opportunity for students to use this time to complete work for their remaining classes.

Remember This

States that require seat time for graduation credit will find this process beneficial in holding students accountable on attendance issues.

Working With Unmotivated Students

The downside to the letter grading system is that grades are an albatross. What a student can do with information is what's important. Reciting facts and numbers is a chain that limits freedom to share, experiment, and explore. Teachers who can create the *want to* in students will increase student interest and willingness to learn and will have fewer disruptive behaviors.

In most educational systems, defiant and disruptive students will receive failing grades and no credit for coming to school or improved behavior or performance. The message to these students is that their effort is not good enough.

We have found that the most unmotivated students will work if they have a say in the process. Getting unmotivated students motivated requires tying their interests and desires to learning opportunities. Unmotivated students do not want to be in a classroom. They don't want to do assignments, and they see little purpose in attending other than staying out of court and the local detention center. Most are compliant if left alone.

Demanding work, giving out Fs, calling home, and sending them to the office or the hallway are the processes that have helped create the unmotivated. They have always been reinforced for poor behavior in the past. We can stop the downward spiral by helping them make sense of why they need to learn for their own benefit. Many of these students are focused on their own needs and are willing to do anything that will benefit them.

A pass/fail grade for these students is recommended. This way the students can obtain credit and advance toward graduation without worrying about their grades; this will bring out the best effort in all students.

> ### Remember This
>
> Unmotivated students will not work for us. They must buy into the idea they are going to get a personal benefit from doing the assignment. We really need to know the culture and nature of the students in order to have the best chance of them doing any work.

Priming the Pump

Getting students to engage in teacher-led class discussions can be one of the toughest tasks to undertake. If students are made to feel nonthreatened, their willingness to participate is increased. We have found that a nonverbal response is one way to get a quantitative response from students. We call it the thumb check.

Here is how it works. Tell the students you are going to take a thumb check regarding information they have recently covered. Let them know that you need their assistance in evaluating if you are on target with their learning. Explain that they will give you a thumb up if they learned anything new or found something interesting, a thumb sideways if they already knew most of the information, and a thumb down if they did not learn anything new. Note: Tell the students that if they do not give you a response you will call on them for a response. All of the students will respond to avoid embarrassment. When the students have shared their responses, inform them what you have learned from their sharing. Finally, ask the students to share what new information they learned, with the understanding that you will not quiz them about their response.

You will be amazed at how this nonverbal thumb check response gets the whole class involved and creates an open discussion.

Reverse Weaning

Teachers want every student to learn, so what can we do? We call the following process *reverse weaning*. As its name suggests, reverse weaning is an attempt to reverse detachment from schoolwork and turn it into attachment to success in school. This is done by rewarding constructive behaviors with personal time, food or video coupons—whatever the student will buy into. Typically, unmotivated students have had so many experiences that fostered poor work habits that their sense of a work ethic is limited. However, if we can show that the work we're requesting benefits them personally, we have a chance of getting them to try. The unmotivated student must be slowly brought to a sense of motivation.

Suggested Rewards

- Tickets and coupons
- Assignments that relate to what the student is interested in—creativity is your ally
- Ten minutes of personal time at his desk in exchange for ten minutes of quality work

Encourage and support whatever effort students put forth. Don't look to grade for quality. Grade based on effort and completion. Then slowly increase time of effort while decreasing external rewards. The student must develop a self-starter attitude.

The EX Bank—A Strategy for Arresting Apathy

Apathy will get in the way of student learning. Creating enticing reasons to perform can get an apathetic student engaged in the learning process. A bailout plan can work for the struggling student, yet bailouts should be used sparingly to avoid conditioning students to believe that subpar work is acceptable on a regular basis (because a bailout will be available later). The challenge of trying to set a personal best or outperform others is enough to get some students to perform. When students are self-motivated for whatever reason, they will perform at amazing levels.

The intervention outlined below offers hope for the struggling student while challenging the self-starter. With this intervention, we have seen the least motivated students rise to levels they never thought possible. Once the students begin to believe in the system, they eagerly look for opportunities to increase their learning.

Creating a situation that allows all students to have control of their grades is a powerful way to build and maintain academic self-starters.

Rationale

If students are engaged and motivated to take control of their grades, they will be less likely to be disruptive. The goal is to encourage and stimulate academic growth. We know students learn in a variety of ways. Hence, how students demonstrate their knowledge is not the focus. The focus is on their continued desire to improve their learning and take ownership for their learning and grades. The primary factor in the EX Bank concept is student control of learning.

How the EX Bank Works

The teacher offers the students an opportunity to obtain extra credit points for doing additional work beyond what is required on daily assignments. Each student's points are then stored in the student's EX Bank account until the student applies the points to a score he wishes to improve. The teacher establishes the boundaries for where and how EX bank points may be applied to a low score. For low-functioning students, it is recommended that teachers allow points to be applied to *any* score. High-functioning students are self-starters and will automatically be drawn toward the EX bank concept, so teachers may use the concept for more specific purposes. For high-functioning students, teachers may wish to establish guidelines for the use of points that meet curricular goals.

EX Bank Deposits

The list below gives examples of work in various subject areas for which students might be given EX Bank points.

Math: **Required** = Ten problems; **EX Bank** = Additional problems.

Science: **Required** = Three experiments; **EX Bank** = Additional experiments.

Reading: **Required** = One chapter; **EX Bank** = Additional chapters or books read.

Physical Education: **Required** = Written tests and demonstrations of skills; **EX Bank** = Additional reports on sports medicine or sports history.

Shop Classes: **Required** = Set number of projects; **EX Bank** = Additional projects and research.

Art: **Required** = Set number of projects; **EX Bank** = Additional projects and research.

Language Arts: **Required** = Set number of essays; **EX Bank** = Additional essays or book reviews.

Social Studies: **Required** = Set projects and assignments; **EX Bank** = Additional research or projects.

Any Class: When students have watched a video in class: **Required** = Set number of notes; **EX Bank** = All the additional notes students come up with (or use the form shown in Figure 5.1).

EX Bank Withdrawals

Remember This

Students included in the establishment of standards will be more likely to be motivated, since they had input into the grading process.

When students turn in extra work, they indicate where they want the points for that work applied. For example, if a student has received a grade of 65% on a test, the student could apply 5 points from the EX Bank to raise the test score to 70%. The teacher should be creative and work with the students to establish the details of where EX Bank points can be applied.

Figure 5.1 Sample EX Bank Form

EX Bank—The Place Where You Control Your Grade

- Additional responses as provided on this form will earn EX Bank points. The number of extra points is shown in parentheses after each category description.

- You may apply your EX Bank points toward *any assignment or project* that you have already turned in and that has received a passing grade.

Title of Presentation _____

Student Name _____

Requirements:

- Each response must be written in complete sentences, must be *numbered to show which category you are addressing,* and must be shown *in columns,* not randomly scattered within the category area.

- Responses should be formatted in 12-point type.

Category 1—Things in the video you found interesting: (5 pts.)

Category 2—Questions you are asking/things you want to know more about: (5 pts.)

Category 3—Cultural characteristics (clothing, food, festivals, traditions) of the time period represented in the video: (3 pts.)

Category 4—What's the most significant thing you learned from the video? (1 pt.)

Recording Points

The rewarding part of the EX Bank for both teacher and student is to sit together and apply points at the student's direction. As students watch their grades improve, a sense of ownership and accomplishment takes place. An efficient approach is for the teacher to provide students with copies of their progress reports and have the students indicate on the reports where they would like their points applied. This allows teachers to adjust the scores in their own gradebooks or grading programs on their own schedule. Teacher should always provide students with updated progress reports after adjustments have been made.

Whether you are using a paper-and-pencil gradebook or an electronic grading program, it is suggested that a category for the EX Bank be set aside without a weighting factor.

Cautions

Students who are accustomed to failure will find it hard to believe they can actually improve their grades by extra effort. They also find it hard to grasp that they are in control of their grades. These students are familiar with failure and need to be encouraged, shown, and guided in order to grasp the concept that they can succeed with additional effort.

Students should never be allowed to use EX Bank points to make up for missing scores (where the student didn't take the test or didn't turn in the assignment), as this undermines the value of assignments, tests, and projects. EX Bank points should not be used to bring a failing score up to a passing score. Tests and assignments to which points are applied should have a base score of at least 65%, or whatever is considered passing. Students must demonstrate a minimum level of understanding to earn the right to improve their grades. This prevents defiant students from loading information of choice into the test and from avoiding using quality study habits. Most teachers develop assessments based on pertinent knowledge necessary for mastery of the discipline being studied. A base standard is therefore required of all students.

Figure 5.1 is an example of a form that could be used by students who want to earn EX Bank points while watching a video or listening to a lecture.

Process and Apply

1. List three academic strategies you will create or modify to address your academic behavior concerns.

2. List and explain five strategies you could use with high-functioning defiant and disruptive students.

3. How could the offering of extra points to bolster a test score encourage the general student population?

4. How could credit appeal hearings serve as a motivator for students to remain in school and improve their academic performance?

5. How would it benefit teachers and students if academic performance contracts and Homework Savers were used in the classroom?

6. Outline a strategy for using the EX Bank concept to motivate students at your instructional level.

7. Explain the value for both student and teacher of knowing student strengths and weaknesses.

8. How could establishing fair and obtainable behavior parameters motivate defiant and disruptive students to succeed academically?

6

Students With Disabilities in the General Education Classroom

A seventh grade math class included a few high-functioning and some low-functioning students. Most of the students were in the middle of the spectrum. The teacher began the year with the idea of teaching to the text. It wasn't long until behavior issues began to surface. The high-functioning students got bored with the simple assignments and blew through the work with ease. When they were finished with an assignment, they would begin to visit and goof around. The low-functioning students were frustrated because they could not finish their assignments in class and had to take them home. The middle group functioned within the teacher's expectations.

After careful thought, the teacher came up with a new delivery process and seating arrangement. For easier management of the groups, high-functioning students were placed on the left side of the room, the middle-level group in the center, and the low-functioning group to the right.

Lessons were addressed to the whole class. After the lesson delivery, high-functioning students were allowed to work at their own pace and ask questions when they needed help. The low-functioning students would get personal assistance. After helping the low-functioning students and getting them going on the assignment, the teacher would monitor the whole class by walking around, checking on assignment progress, and managing behavior.

With this new approach, defiant behavior was kept in check, student performance improved, and learning was maximized. When individual needs were addressed, every student benefited.

Accommodations are missing! Moving from special education to the regular population was an eye opener. When I receive my class roster, there are rarely indicators of a student's accommodations. Based on my background in special education, I am able to figure out when a student is in need of special accommodations. This causes me to wonder about my colleagues' abilities to address student accommodations when they have no information about student accommodations. This is unfair to both teacher and student. It is also a violation of the Individuals with Disabilities Education Act (IDEA).

This chapter in your journey toward successful student management has been written for teachers who have special needs students in their regular education classrooms, but it can also help those whose sole focus is on special needs students. We see various forms of misbehavior stemming from a variety of issues with these students. The chapter will provide some identifying factors that will help teachers decide if a referral for special education services might be in order. In addition, the interventions in this chapter can increase the performance of disruptive and defiant students with special needs while creating a more stable learning environment for the entire class.

Development of Behavioral Disorders

Students with attention deficit disorder (ADD), attention deficit hyperactivity disorder (ADHD), oppositional defiant disorder (ODD), and conduct disorder (CD) have similarities that manifest themselves in common ways. Therefore, these students can be effectively dealt with using strategies that have been found useful with other difficult students. The most important point to remember is that the basic drive of a student with ODD is to resist control and manipulation from any adult (Woolsey-Terrazas & Chavez, 2002). This knowledge is valuable when working with students with ODD and other behavioral disorders.

The research indicates there is a progression in the development of disruptive behavior. According to Dr. David Rabiner of Duke University, "One of the most important things to know about ADHD is that children with ADHD are at increased risk for developing other types of behavior disorders, including Oppositional Defiant Disorder (ODD) and Conduct Disorder (CD)" (Rabiner, 2006, para. 1). This progression is believed to have genetic and neurochemical roots: "Experts believe that ADD has a large genetic component, and is caused by a neuro-chemical disconnection between two parts of the frontal lobes inside the brain. This affects the central nervous system's development, and thus causes impairment in the ability to concentrate" (Amenkhienan, n.d., para. 1). Students born with these chemical deficiencies have a tendency to develop ADD or ADHA. These imbalances are often corrected with medication, but as students with ADD reach the primary school ages of 5 to 10, an increase in disruptive behavior can begin to develop into defiance—ODD. As the student moves through adolescence, there is an increase in conduct disorder—CD (Chandler, n.d.).

After many years of working with students associated with these disabilities, we have observed one thing on a consistent basis. Students challenged about their behavior, and provided choices for better responses to situations that frustrate them, demonstrate fewer outbursts of defiant and disruptive behavior. This leads us to surmise that behaviors that develop beyond the primary ages are learned.

The behavior being learned can also be unlearned through constructive strategies. "Turning around a child with CD is the most rewarding thing a parent or caregiver can do," writes Dr. James Chandler (n.d., In summary, para. 2). Strategies such as those outlined within these pages have caused disruptive and defiant behavior to be reduced or extinguished in students with disabilities.

Disruptive, noncompliant, defiant, and apathetic behavior might be indicators of a learning disability or outside distracters coming from the home or peers. If a consistent pattern of these behaviors exists, it is recommended that the student be referred for further assessment.

Similarly, a consistent pattern of low performance might be an indication that the student does not have the academic skills to accomplish the assigned task. There could be a time management issue in the home or in the student's personal life that needs to be addressed. Exploring through an informal interview with the student can improve performance. Sometimes personal attention is all students need to confirm their value as students and individuals.

Working With Students With Behavioral Disorders

Build a Relationship

Making deposits of encouragement and support help build a relationship that can withstand an emotional withdrawal. Withdrawals come when an unwelcome behavior must be addressed, a major assignment is overdue, a directive from the administration regarding curriculum must take place, or when there are other changes in the learning environment.

Students who have developed trust in their teacher are more likely to accept these withdrawals. Being predictable is the best method for building trust. When students see their teacher as a promise keeper, they too begin to demonstrate that they can be trusted. When teacher and student trust each other, tremendous possibilities emerge.

Another aspect of building relationships is identifying student interests and teaching to them. (See Chapter 1 for some initial approaches to this.) Teaching to a student's interest is always the best way to prevent the disruptive student from taking away instructional time. The research shows that when curriculum has relevance to student interests, students become increasingly motivated to learn. Try to devise examples, case studies, or assignments that relate the course content to students' interests and experiences (Gross Davis, 1993). Underachievement is a complex phenomenon, and interventions to improve student achievement and motivation can be complicated and time-consuming. Student-centered curriculum is a critical ingredient if students are to reach their potential (Ford, Alber, & Heward, 1998).

Provide a Sense of Power and Control

Students who feel they are able to challenge the classroom structure without getting a negative response from the teacher become empowered. They know they can give input and it will be listened to. A sense of shared power is what helps keep the relationship strong and productive. Providing disruptive students some control creates the illusion that they are in control.

There is a set hierarchy in the classroom. The teacher is the leader, and students are expected to follow. Teachers have power and can empower students. The teacher can give up power at appropriate times, creating the illusion that the student is in control. If students believe they have power and control of their learning, both the teacher and the student have achieved the highest level of motivation.

When the teacher gives up power, it empowers the student, and performance increases while disruptions diminish. One approach is to ask questions that give students a sense of power, for example, How would you like to complete your assignment—on the computer, drawing a picture, or creating a poster?

This approach sends a message to the student that they have control of their learning and the power to manage their performance. At first, disruptive students might be abrasive in their attempts at sharing their concerns. However, as they refine their tactics, they feel a sense of power and control as they contribute to the betterment of the classroom. Teachers should make sure their contributions are publicly acknowledged before their peers, staff, and community.

Help Students Make Moral Choices

Forgive Mistakes

The lying nature of students with disorders or disabilities is most often a defense mechanism they have learned for the purpose of protecting themselves from unwanted consequences or embarrassment. Students who are treated with grace and benevolence learn that mistakes happen and will be forgiven. Students who gain trust in their teacher and understand that they will not be chastised for their mistakes develop a sense of hope, and cooperation begins to develop.

Overcome Denial With Trust

Another defensive tactic is to deny ownership of a wrong. As teachers work to gain the trust of their students, defiant students begin to demonstrate confidence in their teachers, and a working relationship begins. Admission of wrong will come more easily for these students, and disruptions will begin to dissipate. Student behavior will begin to take on the form of cooperation and a willingness to take risks in class participation, writing, suggestions, and presentations. Defiant students will no longer desire to disrupt. It's almost as if they don't want to hurt the feelings of the teacher who is working to build the relationship.

Reduce Cognitive Dissonance With Clear Expectations

Being afraid to make a decision is common among students struggling with truth. All students are moral agents and know the social right. What they struggle with is their beliefs about morality. In a society where moral absolutes are weak, students rely on what their environment says is right and wrong. There may be differences between what is expected at home and at school, and the conflict between two competing systems may be confusing. Therefore, it is important to establish class expectations and review them regularly and possibly post them in a visible spot for quick reference.

Hang the Code

Not every situation can be addressed by the classroom rules. The teacher is the monarch in the classroom and can choose to ignore behaviors that would otherwise require a response. Seeking to understand is very important. For example, a student who has never before come late to class, but has been late the last three days in a row, should be interviewed about the tardiness. Although the class rules may state that tardy students will receive a detention, the teacher, upon exploring this student's reason for being tardy, might choose to excuse the tardiness due to extenuating circumstances.

Touch the Soul

Touching the soul with hope and trust will bring out the best in every student. When students understand the classroom expectations, and the expectations are supported with consistency, most students—even those with behavioral disorders—will develop into self-starters and emerge as motivated young men and women able to contribute in the class and society.

Academic Accommodations

Provide a Choice of Assignments

Most students are accustomed to being given directions. This is often where confusion, disruption, defiance, and noncompliance begin. There are many ways for an assignment to be completed— students can give an oral report, provide a written report, participate in a group project, or complete a task electronically on a computer. How students learn is a factor in motivation. Providing alternatives will reduce the desire to sabotage a lesson and encourages students to take the initiative. Students who take control of their learning will be less likely to be a distraction to the learning process.

Allow Students to Redo Assignments

One of the biggest motivators is allowing students to redo assignments. Increased learning takes place, and students feel they have power. Students feel they have won a concession from the teacher because they are getting a second chance at the assignment. In reality, they are picking up additional information and completing a separate assignment that helps them learn what they did not get the first time around.

Help Students Keep Track of Materials

Students with disabilities are known for losing assignments, materials, and books. Setting them up for success allows for a pleasant and productive learning experience for teacher and student. Creating a mutually agreed-upon place for students on individualized education programs (IEPs) to keep their papers and materials prevents needed materials from getting lost. It also creates a relaxing atmosphere when the students know their materials are always in a safe place. We have seen the most disorganized students become motivated and productive as a result of having the needed supplies where and when they need them.

Work With Paraprofessionals and Instructional Aides

Possibly the strongest ally in the classroom is the paraprofessional. These folks are valuable when one-on-one attention is needed. Their training and support can assist the struggling student when the regular teacher is not available. Often these folks have additional insight into special needs students' disabilities and their accommodations. Working with them as team members strengthens the function of the team and delivery for the students they serve.

Strategies for Managing Behavior

Being prepared to address specific behaviors allows the teacher and students the opportunity to be successful. By being prepared, the teacher will be ready to intervene before the class is disrupted. The following list includes examples of preplanning covered elsewhere in this book; all of these are useful in preparing to work with students with disorders and disabilities:

- Seat assignments
- Written and clearly stated expectations and consequences

- Attitude interception at the door
- Reminders of expectations and consequences
- A phone call home requesting support
- Assignment folders that stay in the room
- Creative curriculum alternatives
- Fallback plans

Establish Fair and Obtainable Behavior Parameters

Research demonstrates that the fewer the rules, the more likely students with disabilities are to follow through with expectations (Hoffman Kaser, 2007). Due to lower levels of cognitive understanding, simple and limited expectations with corresponding consequences will give these students a better sense of understanding what is expected of them. The Daily Performance Sheet (see Chapter 3)

> ### Remember This
>
> Mixing up these strategies keeps defiant students off balance. They know defiant behavior will be addressed; they just don't know when and what form it will take.

defines four skills (the four P's) necessary to be productive in the workplace. These basic skills could become the class expectations for both high- and low-functioning students.

In addition, students with IEPs often have behavioral contracts that should be followed. These students should need only a reminder of the expectations and consequences of the IEP.

To establish classroom parameters that are obtainable for all students, it's helpful to evaluate behaviors and consequences in terms of cause and effect: If this happens, then this will happen. Here are some examples:

- If you are tardy to class, you must fill out a CBIP and have it evaluated before you may enter the classroom.
- A yellow card will be administered to disruptive students as a warning. Further disruption will result in a red card and lunch detention.
- If you openly disrupt the class, you will be required to fill out a CBIP before readmittance to the class.
- Continued disruption will result in your removal to the refocus station until you fill out a CBIP and have it evaluated.

These examples take on a progressive sequence and serve as a model for progressive discipline in the classroom. Removal to the hallway or the office is a last resort.

Give Students Responsibilities

Providing disruptive students the opportunity to be part of the class process often gives them opportunity to focus on productive input versus disrupting the class. Some suggestions: leading the flag salute, leading a question-and-answer session, passing out and collecting papers, control of timed periods, and answering the phone.

Teach Problem-Solving Skills

Teaching students that they can choose how to respond provides them options. Younger and emotionally disabled students cannot see beyond the present moment, and they have been preconditioned through their upbringing to respond in given ways based on somebody else's values. Teaching students to explore other options for responding provides them a sense of hope.

Once they begin to develop confidence in decision making and self-advocacy, further assistance needs to be provided through additional training in how to stay calm. Self-paraphrasing their personal thoughts and feelings, before they share them, can help them stop themselves from saying something that might escalate a situation of potential conflict. Journaling is a great way to reinforce what students are learning, and retention increases when they practice writing and processing choices. Learning self-talk and negotiating skills can also be helpful for these students.

Reinforce Expectations

Consistent reinforcement of class expectations is imperative due to the short attention span, lower academic skills, and psychological challenges of students with disabilities and disorders. It is necessary to remind disabled students daily or even several times during a class session what the expectations are.

Provide Immediate Response and Feedback

Research reveals that the closer the feedback is to the time of the assignment, the higher the motivation for learning (Gross Davis, 1993). The greater the motivation for learning, the less time students will spend looking for ways to disrupt the learning process. It is recommended that assignments and assessment results be returned no later than two days after you receive them from students. When an assignment is long or involved, requiring more attention for assessment, it is best to inform the students that the results will be returned later than usual. However, a return date should be given and adhered to. In this respect, teachers need to develop accountability measures for themselves, hence teaching by example. Students who see teachers setting high standards for their own work begin to accept high standards for themselves.

Restrict Passing Time

As was discussed in Chapter 3, sometimes problems can be side-stepped if a particular student is not in the hallway when it is full of students passing between classes. It is highly suggested that when a student is not mature enough to handle movement with the general population, the student be held in the sending classroom until the passing time is over. Then the student may be released to travel empty hallways to the next classroom. If there is suspicion that such students will not go where they are supposed to, an escort needs to be sent with them.

Provide a Personalized Workspace or Tools

Some students need their own tools. Individualized workstations and materials can motivate students to learn. A sense of ownership can create the buy-in a defiant student needs. Defiant students are often self-centered and possessive. Therefore, creating a false sense that they are being considered for special attention—by giving them a personal study area—can prevent additional disruptions.

True Encounter

There was a student who was very disruptive until a special agreement was developed for the student. This student was in a keyboarding class, and he found every way to use the keyboard except for its intended purpose. Why? The student felt inadequate and had given up hope of ever being able to learn how to use the keyboard and its basic functions.

After careful thought, the teacher asked the student if he would mind working in the adjacent room. This room was separated from the keyboarding classroom by a glass wall. This would allow the teacher to keep an eye on the student working next door. The student agreed, with the understanding that he would be able to walk around in his personal room and look out the window, as long as he completed the given assignment each day.

(Continued)

> (Continued)
>
> Result: Classroom interruptions became nonexistent. The isolated student completed every assignment, passed the final test, and received his credit. This student learned that life could be about give and take. He was offered an opportunity to pass the class on his own terms with the teacher's support.

Allow Personal Workspace

Respect for a student's personal workspace encourages trust. Some students don't like the teacher to hover around their desks. Observation from a distance or a casual pass by is often the best way to monitor such students' efforts. The True Encounter below demonstrates how getting to know a student and her personal needs can advance the learning for the student and prevent a class disturbance.

> ### True Encounter
>
> A special needs student did not like the teacher to sit with her to discuss writing corrections. She did not like the teacher to correct her work at her desk. The young lady was also a social butterfly and sought recognition from everyone. What she did like was to ask questions about life and written language.
>
> The teacher agreed to honor the young lady's request to avoid her desk if the girl was willing to limit her chatty behavior by quietly listening to her headphones while she worked on assignments. The young lady agreed, and both she and the teacher were able to accomplish their goals. The teacher had a manageable classroom, and the student asked for help on her own terms when she needed it.
>
> What this did was open the door to better communication between the two, and it improved the writing skills of the student.

Addressing More Severe Behavior Problems

Destruction of School Property

Attention-getting behaviors such as destroying school or personal property might be an indicator of a severe behavior disorder. We have discovered that by tying learning to the offending behavior, a reduction in destructive behavior takes place. The True Encounter below demonstrates the positive effects such a response can have on the classroom.

John was a student who had recently been discharged from a residential center for psychological patients. John's issues manifested themselves in destroying school property, making strange sounds, and running out of the classroom. When John joined a reading class, he was given a book. Several minutes into the class, John began to tear a page out of the book. Although the teacher had anticipated such behavior, he had wanted to give John a chance to make the right decision; when he didn't, the book was quietly removed, and a lap-size whiteboard was given to him. John was informed that he could write questions about the reading on the whiteboard. John proceeded to destroy the marker by forcefully drawing circles and grinding it into the corrugated back side of the whiteboard. Gently, the teacher stated to John that he had drawn a black hole and asked if John knew what a black hole was. John did not know, and a teachable moment occurred. This was a moment to teach proper use of school materials and to work on John's reading, research, writing, and presentation skills.

The teacher told John how black holes were energy fields in space that absorb energy, and how things entering these force fields disappear and are never seen again. His presentation was very animated, kept John's attention, and created curiosity. The presentation was given in such a way that it contained a hint of suspicion indicating that it might not be true. John questioned the teacher about whether it was true. John had taken the bait, so the teacher challenged him to look up "black holes" in the dictionary and write a brief definition on the whiteboard. John did not destroy the dictionary or the new marker he was given. Learning and a connection with the teacher began.

John never again destroyed materials, and he became the leader of the class question-and-answer activities.

Running

Creating a situation that sets the stage for minimal disruptions is always helpful. When teachers are notified that there will be a runner in the class, they are best off assigning the runner to a seat in the corner of the room diagonally opposite the door. This gives them an opportunity to intercept the student in the event of a run attempt. It is further suggested that a conference be held with the student prior to his arrival about what causes him to run. This allows the teacher to monitor the student's environment and make adjustments that can prevent the student from feeling the need to run. If the classroom environment offers more reasons to stay, the student's need to run will diminish.

Violence

When a student with a history of violence exhibits a pattern of socially appropriate behavior (such as may be outlined in the student's IEP and/or classroom expectations), the student should be incorporated into the general population. The violent student is not to be deprived of the least restrictive environment unless it is for the safety of others. But the sanctity of the learning environment is paramount. Students who are often violent should not be allowed to interact with other students on a regular basis.

Helping Students Deal With Anxiety

Working with youngsters can be like working in a dynamite factory: You never know when something is going to blow up. Youngsters in school are dealing with the most stress they have known in their young lives. Many are overwhelmed with what they face. Hence, a short fuse is a given.

Private discussions with students about their anxiety provide them with the respect they deserve until they are able to face what is causing the fear. Exploring their fears with them allows them to begin the process of breaking down what brings on their anxiety. Facing their fears—by stating what the fears are—allows the students to better deal with the fear when it surfaces.

A good way to start is to ask students at what point they start to feel anxious. Finding out what causes the feeling of anxiousness provides you with the needed information to establish an environment that can alleviate the fears that lead to anxiety. Writing contractual agreements can also help; they empower students to effectively deal with their fears. The strategies developed in such contracts enable anxious students to more effectively handle their fears when they surface.

Background Music and Sounds

We have also noticed that recorded background sounds, such as the sounds of ocean waves, a swamp, a jungle, or chimes, have a calming effect on anxious students. Background sounds have proven effective during instruction as well as study time. Light jazz has also been effective. The most effective use has been during study time. We have had many students request the sounds or music be turned on. They have stated it helps them focus. The most effective use of this intervention has been with students with behavior disorders in classes for students with special needs.

Stress Pass

There are students who have not arrived at the point where they can manage their emotions without assistance. Giving such students a Chill Pass or Stress Pass can assist them in monitoring their own emotions. When students with a pass begin to feel anxious, they can use the pass to remove themselves from the learning environment. The pass should have directions written on it as to

> **Remember This**
>
> We can light the fuse with a thoughtless comment or action. Knowing what lights each student's fuse is power.

where students are to report when they leave class—typically to a trusted staff member or the office. The emphasis is to give them a chance to work through their stress and then return to the learning environment.

True Encounter

Brandon had been classified as having anxiety disorder, ODD, high-functioning Asperger syndrome, and ADHD. Brandon liked to use his anxiety disorder classification to get out of doing work and being able to shut down when he wanted.

Brandon was spoken to in private by his teacher about his anxiety and was informed that everyone has anxiety. He was told that having anxiety isn't the problem; it's how one deals with it.

The teacher asked Brandon what made him anxious. Brandon confessed that he did not like having a one-on-one paraprofessional following him around because other students made fun of him. The teacher asked Brandon if it would help if the services of the paraprofessional were removed from the IEP. Brandon said it would.

The teacher called for a multidisciplinary team meeting to discuss Brandon's needs. Brandon's mother agreed to a two-week trial period without the paraprofessional. After Brandon went two weeks with no incidences and improved classroom performance, the paraprofessional was reassigned. Brandon went on to become a successful student, passed all sections of the state assessment test for his grade level, and needed only one period daily in the resource room—to work on his writing.

Brandon never again demonstrated anxiety and did not use this classification to avoid schoolwork.

Addressing Cognitive Disabilities

Adjust the Workload to the Ability of the Student

IDEA—the Individuals with Disabilities Education Act—assures all students that they will be educated *at their ability levels.* Identifying this level for each student and adjusting the work to it has often been frustrating for general education teachers, parents, students, aides, and special needs staff. Adjusting the workload requires additional planning; the modifications might include allowing students to do fewer or shorter assignments or tests, or providing an aide or a student to read material aloud to them, write for them as they dictate, or assist them in other ways.

It is not necessary to write separate assignments for special needs students. A reduction in the standard assignment is all that is needed. With the reductions in the assignments, special needs students should not need additional time. If they do, make arrangements for them to complete the work during their time in the resource room or after school at home. A sample of student work meets the IEP expectation, and that sample is enough to evaluate the student's ability.

Scoring should be based on the same standard that is used for other students. In other words, if an IEP student scores 77% on a reduced assignment, the score recorded for the student should be 77%, just as it would be for a non-IEP student who scores 77% on the full assignment.

Because public education is moving ever closer toward the inception of IEPs for *all* students—not just those identified as having special needs—it would behoove the general education teacher to begin tailoring lessons for individual students and/or for groups of students with similar needs.

> **Remember This**
>
> Special needs students at the secondary level often function at a much lower level (comparable to that of students of primary school age) than their chronological age would suggest.

Know Student Strengths and Weaknesses

As you get to know your students, you will be able to design lessons that capitalize on their strengths and provide interventions for their weaknesses. This process demonstrates genuine care for each student. In addition, preparing ahead of time and meeting your students at the door, as described for all students in Chapter 4, is particularly useful with special education students. Remove the guessing and reduce lost instruction time by knowing as much as you can about each student's attitude, energy, and emotions before students come into the classroom. Knowing what they are bringing to the class will dictate how you deliver your lesson.

Use a Scribe

Scribes for students with dysgraphia and dyslexia can be beneficial. Using an Alpha Smart Word Processor can also be useful. When the scribe is another student, scribing can be beneficial for the scribe and the needy student. Student scribes need to have a higher focus than most other students, because the students they are scribing for depend on them for accuracy—a needy student's success is dependent on the scribe. Scribes find a sense of pride because they have an additional sense of accomplishment in seeing their classmates excel due to their contributions.

Vary Lesson Presentation

As varied as students' lives are, so are their learning styles and their abilities to learn. Students are survivors. They will find a way to accomplish the assignments. The teacher needs to be observant and take careful note as to how each student learns. One visual learner will not see the demonstration the same as another. Therefore, it is a good idea to present each lesson in several different ways.

We have observed students who inhale assignments while others are still trying to figure out what page to be on. Both types of students can do quality work and be productive. They just move at different speeds. For classrooms that include students with a wide range of learning speeds, it is suggested that two lessons be prepared: Lesson A will be

Remember This

Assessing the student's learning style provides the teacher valuable information in planning lessons that have the best chance of being received well by the student. This will create an enjoyable learning environment for both teacher and student.

Remember This

Not all students are capable of working at the same rate.

Remember This

Granite can only be shaped into a beautiful monument one chisel cut at a time.

All of what has been suggested takes a tremendous amount of time and energy. The result is that students become self-starters. Are there model students? Yes, because someone took extraordinary time to help develop each of them. It might have been the home environment and expectations, or it might have come from a teacher who challenged the student to rise above mediocrity.

for the entire class, while lesson B will be for those who have completed lesson A. Lesson B holds extra value and encourages the more advanced student to gain additional learning. This approach also encourages students to move a little faster on Lesson A.

Process and Apply

1. Create a list of indicators that will help you determine if a student needs special accommodations.

2. List three ways the Student Learning Survey or 3 × 5 Card (see Chapter 2) can assist a teacher of special needs students.

3. Given the view of Wendy Woolsey-Terrazas and Janice A. Chavez, what would be the most effective approach for working with ODD students who resist authority and manipulation?

4. How could the strategies listed in the Strategies for Managing Behavior work to deter defiant students?

5. How could adjusting the workload to the ability of the student serve as a motivator for struggling students?

7

Building Winning Relationships

Jerrod had a self-inflicted learning disability due to excessive huffing of spray paint. He was living with his mother and her boyfriend on the first floor of their house while his father lived on the second floor with his girlfriend. Jerrod was 16 and the father of a two-year old-daughter. The mother of his daughter was a middle school student.

My first encounter with Jerrod was to enquire why he was not doing his assignment. He responded with an obscenity while glaring into my eyes; I ignored the obscenity and walked away. The resulting look on Jerrod's face will forever be impressed on my mind. It was a look of bewilderment and confusion. I truly believe he was accustomed to being scolded, kicked out of class, or referred to the office. After that initial encounter, I modified all other inquiries about his schoolwork to compliment him for any signs of effort or to ask him if he needed any assistance.

As time passed, Jerrod began to seek out my help. He also became an ally for enforcing classroom expectations and would challenge other students to get in line. Jerrod enjoyed power sports and was a big NASCAR fan. We were able to have quality discussions about future plans, his daughter, and his relationship with his girlfriend. Jerrod would ask for my advice about decisions he had to make and would ask what I would do. Eventually he brought his daughter by my room to introduce her to me and left a picture of him and her for my Wall of Fame, where I post school pictures, cartoon drawings, outstanding work, and so forth. (This is a spot where students are promoted publicly at their request or by teacher choice. It's a great way to keep student motivation high.) Jerrod graduated from regular high school while awaiting the birth of his second child by the same girlfriend.

Building relationships is about providing a second chance for students most of us give up on. Not every student wants to be rescued, nor can they all be, but our journey to successful student management includes reaching out to all of them.

Essentials for Working With Disruptive and Defiant Students

Trust

Students must be able to count on teachers to do what they say they will do: to enforce expectations regarding discipline, to conduct class activities as they said they would, and to keep promises. Consistency is vital in building trust. Whether the student agrees with the teacher is not the issue. What is imperative is that the student be able to anticipate the teacher's response.

In addition, unconditional acceptance of student behavior allows the student to develop trust in the teacher. Trust will lead to compliance and cooperation from the student.

> **Remember This**
>
> These lines—my own paraphrases from the biblical book of Corinthians—summarize what is necessary to build good relationships with students:
>
> Love is patient, kind, protects, trusts, hopes, is truthful, and perseveres.
>
> Love is not rude, self-seeking, or easily angered; it keeps no record of wrong.
>
> Loving persons treat others the way they want to be treated.

Respect

In American culture, respect must be earned. It is no longer a right. Teachers earn students' respect when teachers are open and honest, and when they are willing to give students as much control over their learning as the students are capable of. Are we willing to openly admit error? Are we willing to accept that a student might know something we don't? Are we willing to let a student teach or take limited control?

Students make mistakes. When the teacher looks for ways to acknowledge their efforts, rather than their errors, the student begins to develop respect for the teacher. When students irritate the teacher and the teacher's response is with calm and grace, the student usually begins to respond in a like manner.

Note: Some students have been deprived of respect for so long that they rarely if ever provide reciprocal respect. Some have become morally bankrupt and callused. Nevertheless, the class is best served if the teacher treats *all* students with respect, whether they learn to reciprocate or not.

Kindness

Genuine compassion in the form of gentle greetings and unexpected rewards increases student willingness to meet classroom expectations.

Positive Approaches That Build Relationships

Consider the following precepts as methods and strategies that can aid in building and strengthening teacher and student relationships.

Tact

In *Webster's New World Dictionary* (3rd college edition, 1988), *tact* is defined as "delicate perception of the right thing to say or do without offending." This is possible if the proper parameters are set beforehand—that is, if rules and expectations are established at the beginning of a relationship—so teachers can render an ultimatum tactfully by referring back to the expectations and pointing out how current behavior varies from them.

Tact also manifests itself in the teacher's efforts to build trust and respect and to discipline and coach from a distance. Being gentle yet firm, using gentle words to turn away wrath, and allowing some give and take are further manifestations of a teacher's tactfulness. All these approaches provide guidance while protecting students' feelings and confirming their integrity.

A Quiet Voice

A loud voice and shouting across the room agitate students and disrupt the learning environment. It is recommended that this type of behavior be used only in limited situations. Limited use of a raised voice will get the needed reaction at the appropriate time. If it is used too often, students become desensitized and unresponsive, causing anxiety for teacher and students to rise.

Gentle Yet Firm

Quiet encounters at the student's desk are a good approach to making instructional adjustments to student work. This prevents embarrassment, fosters trust, and opens dialogue. A gentle and controlled voice confirms the standards of the learning environment and sends the message of who is in control while maintaining the dignity of the student.

Gentleness is not a sign of weakness. It affirms the value of the students and assures them of their worth. Students understand genuine concern spoken gently. The most angered student can be subdued with a gentle word spoken sincerely.

Establishing student worth in the classroom provides opportunities to be firm when needed. Gentleness is sufficient to reestablish the learning environment during minor disruptions. When the need to be firm occurs, and students need to be reminded of the educational purpose for which they are there, firmness establishes control and provides an atmosphere of predictability.

Firmness does not have to be a demonstration of authoritarian control. Societal roles of teacher and student are understood. The teacher is monarch and has ultimate control of the classroom. Students will become willing subjects when they know they are cared for and have a voice in what takes place in the classroom. This working relationship promotes stability, respect, and a productive learning environment. How soon these attributes are part of the classroom framework depends on how soon and how often students are treated with tact and respect, and on how soon teachers can demonstrate that they can be trusted to keep their word and enforce classroom rules.

Body Language

This is important in establishing trusting relationships. Much has been said about touching students. A gentle pat on the shoulder or a handshake works wonders for most students. Touching must be reciprocal or avoided.

Correction Versus Control

Correction is part of the academic process. When a student needs to be reminded of expectations, having the student share what the expectations are can best reinforce the expectations. If the student is not able or willing to define the expectation, then it is time for reteaching. Have the student search for the established expectation by asking other students or reviewing the class guidelines.

The ultimate goal is to guide the student toward academic and social growth. Gentle correction along the way encourages students to take ownership in their development. Correction provides the opportunity for the teacher and student to work together as coworkers.

Correcting a student is different from control. Control does not allow students to make choices for self-improvement. The main purpose behind control is to create a situation where the teacher can manipulate student behavior, usually through the threat of negative consequences if submission to the teacher's authority is challenged.

Genuine Interest in Students

Taking a personal interest in students is one of the best deterrents to defiant behaviors. Gaining insight into a student's personal life allows the teacher and student to gain a greater understanding for each other, and it provides for tolerance and understanding when the student becomes disruptive or defiant. Learning how a student connects to life will allow the teacher to align lessons with student interests. What's causing the misbehavior can be learned by getting to know your students. Here are some things you might discover:

- Not all students like themselves, and acting out may be a self-directed attempt to sabotage any help they might receive.
- Attacks on others are often misdirected anger. Any available target will do. If you understand what might be behind your student's anger, you can be ready to dispense an equal amount of compassion as a counter to the student's frustration. As we've said before, a gentle word turns away wrath.

We can get to know our students by assisting at their desks, visiting in the hallway, talking to other staff members, and talking to parents and guardians. All of these efforts create avenues and open doors that will prove to be valuable when working together in the classroom.

Visiting students outside the school setting goes a long way toward building bridges with them. Visits to them in the hospital; attendance at family and community functions such as funerals, bar mitzvahs, confirmations, and weddings; and attendance at extracurricular activities related to school and outside school (4H, Future Farmers of America, Future Business Leaders of America, sports, civic performances, church) can pay big dividends when it comes time to confront a student demonstrating unacceptable behavior.

Getting into a student's personal life has other advantages as well. It enables students to gain a greater understanding of us as well as enabling us to gain a greater understanding of them. Learning how students connect to life will also allow us to align lessons with student interests. It is our responsibility to teach students wherever they are in their journeys through life. Learning to understand their feelings, beliefs, interests, emotions, circumstances, families, and culture (essentially everything about them) will demonstrate that we care. Once students know we truly care, they will begin to cooperate with us.

Where does this type of interaction lead? Sometimes students return to visit teachers years later to share their appreciation for what the teachers did and said when they worked together.

True Encounter

Joe was a disinterested and disruptive student. It seemed his mind was always somewhere else, thinking about something other than school. I started to observe his behavior a little more closely and began noticing that he wore shirts and jackets that promoted drag racing.

During a parent meeting, his mother mentioned that Joe was involved in drag racing, and his grandfather was his sponsor. I asked her when and where Joe would be racing next. I enjoy power sports and had a personal interest in what Joe was involved in.

My wife and I went to one of the races and discovered several very important things. Joe's younger brother, who would later become a student at my school, was also sponsored by their grandfather. Joe's grandfather is one of the wealthiest farmers in the valley and has flown the town's legendary high school football coach to college games so the coach can watch his sons play. I also learned that Joe's father was involved in drag racing.

When Joe figured out I was interested in power sports *and* education, a bond of trust and understanding developed between us. The result was that Joe had a greater interest in school and reduced disruptions.

Greeting Students at the Door

Greeting students at the door was discussed in earlier chapters as a way to set up a positive classroom environment and head off problems before they enter the classroom. It also serves to provide a brief chance to check in on their personal lives. This not only gives you a window into their lives, it also helps keep the focus on school once the student enters the classroom.

This greeting at the door is particularly important when students are returning from a suspension. Debriefing prior to reentry is important in clarifying expectations and clearing up any misunderstandings. Student success is based upon a mutual effort toward the academic goals of the class. Taking time to reestablish the relationship is beneficial in building trust and support for the student.

Affirmation as Young Adults

Youngsters have a desire to be recognized as young adults.

When a teacher is in the presence of young people or talking about them to others, it's affirming to refer to them as young adults. It's amazing how much more attentive they become when acknowledged as young adults.

Addressing preadolescents and adolescents as young adults is a winner every time. Young people desire to be associated with adults more than with children. They have spent the first 12 years of life being referred to as children, and they have been looking forward to becoming older persons. Affirming their desire to be accepted by the adult world as a young adult gives them a sense of being accepted by adults as they mature. As awkward as young people are at figuring out how to perform as an adult, confirming they are on their way helps build the relationship.

Similarly, students appreciate being referred to as ladies or gentlemen. Young people might not act like ladies and gentlemen; however, this should not deter adults from addressing them as such. This address affirms that they should behave as adults. This works better than saying "Quiet down" or "Listen up."

Honoring Accomplishment

Looking for ways to promote students is a great way to build relationships. In class, recognition through coupons, rewards, and public recognition is highly recommended. When the teacher gets the chance to publicly recognize students at assemblies and in the local news, students' sense of self-worth increases, and mutual respect grows between students and teachers.

Special Considerations for the Introvert Student

Introvert actions come into play if the student wants to be left alone. Sometimes we get the feeling these students want little attention, so we focus on them briefly to avoid embarrassing them. For example, make a joke or mention something funny, and then, when the introvert student doesn't respond, call their bluff by saying, "Now don't laugh. Don't laugh." Students usually cannot hold back their laughter, and the barriers begin to come down.

Taking attendance on the first day by visiting students at their desks creates a sense of trust. The introvert prefers this practice because it reduces public attention, which the introvert does not want. These one-on-one approaches often create a comfort zone that causes the student to feel safe, leading the student to participate in class discussions and bringing about opportunities for future personal attention.

Remember This
Some extrovert students will try to take advantage of privileges. Make their assistance in these activities conditional, based on being cooperative and earning the privilege.

Special Considerations for the Extrovert Student

Extroverts have a need to be the focus of attention, so we give it to them by providing them the stage. For example, we might ask these students to hand out papers, lead the flag salute, read the bulletin, or give answers to an assignment from the teacher's key. The bond of trust usually begins when the student gets attention.

Communicating Effectively

Communicating to build winning relationships requires asking a key question: How will the recipient receive my comment? The answer is dependent upon your knowledge of the student. Particularly with defiant students, the frail relationship needs to be nurtured and protected. The defiant student has learned through life that trust is not given easily to anyone. Therefore, you must work exceptionally hard to maintain what you and the student have worked so hard to develop. What might seem like an insignificant situation or comment for most students might be just the reason for the defiant student to believe that trust has been violated once again.

Each student requires a different approach. As unique as student personalities are, so are their needs. Students come to our classrooms with a myriad of issues, values, and beliefs.

> **True Encounter**
>
> Scores were low on the quiz that had been used as an entry activity, and the teacher was frustrated at the level of apathy and low retention from the prior day's lesson. The teacher expressed concern for the general performance of the class and asked for their suggestions as to how to improve scores. The students suggested adding an EX Bank question to the usual three entry quiz questions, and allowing a correct answer to the EX Bank question to take the place of an incorrect answer to the entry quiz questions.

Six Rules for Effective Communication

These rules form a good summary of the steps to effective communication that have been discussed in many places throughout this book:

1. Ask

2. Listen

3. Mutual solutions/negotiate

4. Observe

5. Adjust

6. Apologize

What Works After the Relationship Is Built

These strategies do work when a solid foundation has been established between student and teacher. They can and have had the reverse effect with students who do not know or trust the teacher.

No Student Wants to Be Embarrassed

"Don't make me do what I don't want to do." This statement does two things. First, it causes the student to stop and wonder what the teacher is talking about. Second, the student reflects on what she should be doing. This usually creates a situation where the student will make the choice that aligns with classroom expectations.

It may also be useful to ask, "Do you really want to do that?" The goal is to get students to make choices that align with the classroom expectations. Keep asking questions that trigger guided choices toward the direction you desire. Other examples include, "Are you making the best choice?' and "Are you willing to live with your decision?" After they have heard these questions a few times, disruptive students will begin to make the preferred decision prior to your involvement.

Humor

The teacher who laughs with the students builds solid relationships. Teachers must learn to laugh with students and allow students to see them in a natural light.

But humor can also be dangerous, even with the most trusting of students. Humor can put the teacher on the same level as the students and can be unhealthy if left unchecked. The teacher should always maintain the higher standard and set the tone for acceptable behavior. This is not to say that laughter and laughing should be avoided. Laughter is a beneficial tool in any environment, but it should be monitored and used in a timely manner. Some students are prone to laughter and a giddy personality. Remind students that there is a time for such behavior.

True Encounter

In the earlier years of my teaching, I served as a volunteer fire fighter. I was teaching a seventh grade math class at the time, and I often found it helpful to share stories with my students about emergency calls I had participated in. On one particular call, a young girl had been climbing a tree when she slipped and wedged her knee between two of the tree's limbs. She could not go up or pull her leg out. I had to climb up the tree and, using all my strength, I separated the limbs just enough to free her leg. Once the girl was free, her mom brought out cookies and gave all the fire fighters hugs.

All of my seventh grade students had their own opinions about the situation. Many of the student comments created laughter as well as criticism toward the young girl, and I had to monitor the comments to avoid going into inappropriateness.

This form of personal revelation about my life outside the classroom opened additional opportunities to share and grow as a class. Many life lessons were learned, and an open relationship emerged with the students. Additionally, the fire fighter experiences became a source of motivation. Students knew that a story would be told if the class was on track and everyone was working.

Be Transparent and Human

Students expect teachers to set the standards for the classroom. There are unspoken understandings about the roles of teacher and student. With those understandings, it is helpful to remain transparent. When students feel their teachers are not being themselves, this often is understood as a sign that the teacher is insecure, and it opens the door for the disruptive student to look for ways to attack the teaching process.

Teachers who are transparent earn respect and trust from their students. If teachers are at peace with themselves, the students will also begin to have a sense of peace. The True Encounter about my fire fighting also served as an example of my own transparency. Other examples might include anything the teacher feels comfortable sharing, for example, the death of a favorite pet or family member, a personal injury or accident, and travel experiences. These opportunities work best when they come up spontaneously. Planned sharing can come across as forced and unnatural. The teacher should be cognizant of the teachable moment that connects real life to the lesson, and be masterful enough to blend the two while managing the opportunity to avoid a derailment from the lesson.

> **Remember This**
>
> Once the relationship is established through mutual respect, students begin to manage themselves and those around them. This is paradise for the teacher. It takes work and determination to get there, yet it's worth every minute spent.

Emotional Banking—A Concept for Understanding Relationships

We live in a period of student rights. In order to maintain professional dignity and classroom control, we must invest in the student. Students can be invested in through compliments and genuine care. Compliments are easy and go a long way in building a relationship. These are what we call emotional "deposits." When the time comes to introduce something the students might resist, we can count on those deposits to accomplish our goals.

When an emotional "withdrawal" is necessary, the proper framing of the communication is vital. Gentle words spoken firmly convey a message of seriousness, and that deliberate action needs to be taken. Most students will understand a disciplinary directive is necessary when they have been the recipient of supporting words and acts in the past. The bigger the emotional bank account, the bigger the withdrawal can be when needed.

This concept can be used even to understand authoritarian relationships, but we call this "poverty" emotional banking, because the relationship does not have the depth of trust, respect, and kindness that allows for maximal student learning and growth. In these impoverished relationships, emotional deposits and withdrawals are authoritarian; they lack empathy and mutual respect.

Poverty Emotional Banking—What Works?

Deposits	Withdrawals
1. Appreciation for humor and entertainment provided by the individual	1. Put-downs or sarcasm about the individual
2. Acceptance of what the individual cannot say about a situation	2. Insistence on and demands for a full explanation
3. Respect for the demands and priorities of relationships	3. Insistence that our own situation is the norm and correct
4. Using the adult voice	4. Using the parent voice

Source: Adapted from Payne, 2005.

In contrast, what we call "middle-class" emotional banking reflects much deeper, mutually respectful relationships, in which students feel comfortable in school and are able to learn best.

Middle-Class Emotional Banking—What Works?

Deposits	Withdrawals
1. Seeking first to understand	1. Seeking first to be understood
2. Keeping promises	2. Breaking promises
3. Kindnesses, courtesies	3. Unkindnesses, discourtesies
4. Clarifying expectations	4. Violating expectations
5. Being loyal to the absent (not talking behind anyone's back)	5. Disloyalty, duplicity
6. Apologies	6. Pride, conceit, arrogance
7. Being open to feedback	7. Rejecting feedback

Source: Adapted from Covey, 1989.

Teachers will naturally want to avoid any of the behaviors in the *Withdrawals* column in this chart (although they may be forgiven for the occasional lapse), but their students will perceive disciplinary action as a withdrawal, so teachers will want to make as many deposits as they can to counteract whatever withdrawals they need to make.

> **Remember This**
>
> Sarcasm and rudeness can destroy all positive interaction and emotional deposits. They are huge emotional withdrawals with most students.

Finding the Positive to Deposit Into the Bank

Consider the phrase, "You think you're smart when you answer questions, but we think you're smart when you ask questions." Students may not be willing to take the risk of asking questions, let alone answering questions, for fear of drawing attention to themselves. Many youngsters are comfortable staying back in the pack, so how do we draw them out into the open to take the risk? The best way is to ensure that any feedback is acceptable.

It is the task of the teacher to search student comments and keep the comments connected to the lesson. This is an art that takes practice, but with such practice, the most off-track comments can be used to create positive outcomes. The result: Student responses are affirmed, their dignity is kept intact, and future prospects for additional contributions are heightened.

How to Turn a No Into a Yes

Inside every student's response to a question is an element of correctness. It is the teacher's responsibility to turn an incorrect response into a moment of hope for the student who took a risk in front of his peers to answer a question. Here is an example of how this is done:

Teacher: "Where was the War of 1812 fought?"

Student: "After the American Revolution."

Teacher: "That's right. It was after the American Revolution. Now can you tell me where the war was fought?"

Student: "Uhhhh? 1812?"

Teacher: "Right. The war was fought in 1812. Was the war fought in the United States, England, France, or on the open seas?"

Student: "Oh yeah! It was fought on the open seas of the Atlantic and in the United States."

Teacher: "You're right! The War of 1812 was fought on the Atlantic and in the United States."

Class Environments That Foster Winning Relationships

Maintaining Dignity for Everyone

Preservation of students' dignity should be one of the highest goals of a teacher. Students who know a teacher will put the student's interest above their own will take risks and not fear that their attempt will be rejected. Knowing a teacher will defend a student's dignity will encourage students to contribute.

Among the biggest challenges teachers face are the put-downs of one student to another, or group attacks on an individual. When students are made to feel embarrassed, they will usually respond with laughter, a physical outburst, withdrawal, or crying. Each of these responses will lead to a disruption in the learning process. When such a challenge puts a student's dignity on the line, it is the teacher's duty to stop the assault as soon as it surfaces. To ignore the behavior sets up the class for future disturbances.

A Productive Palace, Not a Permissive Prison

Permissiveness is defined as giving freedom, not being strict or lenient. But when the teacher takes a laissez-faire approach to classroom management and student responses, the class can be a prison of sorts. This environment causes struggling students to feel imprisoned. The teacher offers little support for all members of the class and has a tendency to focus on the more assertive ones. A form of isolation begins to take place for students whose learning style does not match this permissive teaching style, and they don't want to be in class.

When students don't want to be somewhere, they will begin to alter the setting into something they perceive to be worthy of their time. An educational setting in which there is freedom to choose from a defined set of options based on students' various learning styles will become a welcome place where students want to be, a type of palace. A productive environment provides hope for every student.

The classroom is then a safe place to be and a welcomed haven for all students. This type of classroom might be the only place where struggling students feel safe during the day.

Consistency

Consistency will provide a stable and predictable learning environment. One of the characteristics of a successful classroom is the students' ability to predict in what direction the class is headed. Consistency provides a sense of calm and understanding, while taking away guessing and confusion. In order to maximize predictability and thus instructional time, a set daily schedule is suggested.

Students who experience a high level of consistency from the teacher will rise to the teacher's expectations. When asked what the class expectations are, a student should be able to give a reasonable response that is relatively close to what the teacher expects. If the student has a limited idea, it might be because the teacher has not communicated the expectations clearly, frequently, and consistently.

Making Yourself Obsolete

Students who willingly follow lesson plans and classroom procedures in the absence of the teacher are self-starters. They can and will take ownership for their behavior; therefore, the ultimate goal is to guide students in such a way that they become self-starters. This takes place through consistent classroom operations, clear expectations, and opportunities for the students to practice the expected behaviors when in and out of the teacher's presence.

To develop self-starters, you must first teach them how to fly. Teachers should allow their students the freedom to take control of their learning and environment. Giving them short periods of time to work without supervision, and then progressing into longer segments, will encourage strong study habits and time management. Incorporating these strategies with the personal accountability of the Daily Performance Sheet will prepare students to be high-functioning individuals as they move into higher levels of learning.

Conducting the class themselves, in the absence of the teacher, affirms that the students have the ability to work on their own. It's interesting how many students actually function amazingly well when left alone for short periods of time.

True Encounter

One year I taught a class of students with behavioral disorders. One day I was absent, and the substitute teacher did not arrive. I had placed the lesson plans on my desk with clearly marked instructions.

As the students entered the class, one student turned on the overhead projector that showed the entry activity for the day. Since the students were conditioned to do an entry activity as soon as they entered the class, they began working on it. As some of the students began to finish the activity, and assuming I was being delayed, a student went to my desk to see if there was an assignment. The student found the assignment for the class and distributed it to his classmates with the instructions.

The class conducted themselves in a professional manner, completed and collected the assignments, and placed the assignments on my desk. It was interesting to learn that the most defiant student did not do the entry activity or the assignment, even at the pleading of classmates. But even so, no student left during the 80-minute class.

I returned the next day with amazement and praise for the students. An appreciation party was catered by one of the moms, and the article below was written for the local newspaper.

THE SEATTLE TIMES Local/Regional TUESDAY MAY 10, 2004

Student teacher: Ben Torres, a sophomore at Skyline High School in Sammamish, doubled as a teacher during second period recently.

A substitute teacher was supposed to take over Rich Korb's world geography class. The teacher didn't get there.

"When the class realized that no one was coming, Ben found the lesson plans I had laid out on my desk," said Korb in a letter he wrote to Torres' parents.

"He took roll, passed out the worksheets, started the video, and collected the completed worksheets at the end of class."

What's even more impressive was the class itself: Not a single student left the room.

During the period, a couple of educational assistants came by and saw the class watching the video and taking notes.

At the end of the period, another teacher stopped by to check on the class and discovered Torres had handled everything.

"What's amazing," Korb said, "is that this was an extended (80-minute) period, which is a stretch for most students and staff."

Last week when Korb returned to the classroom, he gave Torres a fast-food gift certificate and threw a party for the entire second-period class for their impressive performance.

Source: Grindeland, 2004. Used with permission.

Students Will Take Ownership for Their Behavior

As this story shows, youngsters should not be underestimated regarding their ability to control themselves or their learning environment. Believing that youngsters will always rise to the challenge, when given the opportunity, goes a long way in building trust and productivity.

Students are also capable of making constructive decisions regarding their learning. It's impressive when students request to sit in the hall or quietly listen to their headphones so they can study in isolation or to avoid conflicts with other students. Negotiations should be open when these requests are made. But the teacher might be preparing to present important information all students need to hear, so it would be appropriate to inform such students that they can work in the hall, or quietly listen to their headphones, after they have heard the lesson.

When there have been deposits to the student's emotional bank, this negotiation can be favorable for both the teacher and the student. A win-win outcome has occurred, and an additional emotional deposit has been made. The teacher who practices and refines the above process will gain additional respect from the class, student body, administration, and community.

> **Remember This**
>
> To facilitate students becoming self-starters, be prepared to supply the needed tools. Once students become familiar with the classroom environment and know where supplies and materials are located, they are able to cooperate and organize themselves into constructive activities.

How You'll Know When You Have Built Winning Relationships

> **Remember This**
>
> When students are treated well, respected, and encouraged, and when the work has meaning, high levels of motivation will automatically develop.

- Do students always seem to be hanging around your room?
- Do students come to confide in and visit with you?
- Do students find it easy to talk with you during class?
- Can students predict your responses to statements and questions?
- Do students acknowledge you in a friendly manner outside the school setting?

True Encounter

In the early hours before school began, a counselor brought a young man to the locker room. The counselor stated that the young man needed a place where he could take a shower. His stepfather would not allow him to address personal hygiene at home. As the weeks passed and the young man came in regularly to shower, he began to share his frustrations about his stepfather. He was not allowed to be home alone with his stepsisters, he was ridiculed for being concerned about hygiene, and he could only be at home when his mother was present.

The young man found a listening ear with one of the teachers and began to accept the advice he was being given. Putting the advice into action helped the young man change his focus.

One morning the young man shared that his life had taken a tremendous turn for the better. He stated that while he was jogging with his mother, he had made a decision to take a different path than the one he was on. He and his mother began to go to church, they moved away from the stepfather, and they started life over with a different point of view.

The young man moved on to high school, and the teacher lost track of the student. In the young man's senior year, he returned to the school where the teacher had befriended him. The young man informed the teacher that he was now the student body president at the high school and leader of a Bible study group. He had returned to say, "Thanks for taking the time to help me out."

Another student was on his way to prison and stopped by the school for encouragement and advice. Another student looked up his old teacher to seek advice about marriage. Another student athlete showed up at a football game to share his future plans.

All four of these students had become allies of the teacher and helped keep unruly students in check when they were in school. They continued to seek and use the teacher's advice in their adult lives.

Investing in students provides rewards in and out of the classroom.

A Parting Thought

There will come times when you will ask yourself, Are my attempts to help students really making a difference? The answer is yes. But for the vast majority of our students, we cannot know what that difference is. A way to make peace with our efforts and identify what we can hope for is found in the extract below, from the work of renowned motivational speaker Zig Ziglar:

> You were born to win, but to be a winner, you must plan to win, prepare to win, and expect to win.

You are the only person on earth who can use your ability.

You've got to "be" before you can "do," and you've got to "do" before you can "have."

Your attitude, not your aptitude, will determine your altitude.

When you put faith, hope, and love together, you can raise positive kids in a negative world. (Ziglar, 1985)

Process and Apply

1. List three consequences of not apologizing when you have made an error.

2. Why would it be beneficial to handle an introvert student differently than an extrovert?

3. Explain how each of the six rules for effective communication can assist you in working with a defiant or disruptive student.

4. How can an understanding of poverty, as defined in terms of poverty emotional banking by Dr. Ruby Payne, prevent you from insisting that your way is the only way to run the classroom?

5. What is meant by the statement, "To develop self-starters, you must first teach them how to fly"?

8

Concluding Thoughts

The journey is just beginning! What? You thought we were done! But now you have new ideas for traveling the path to successful student management, and we hope you feel energized to begin anew to take on the most challenging students. This concluding chapter will give you an opportunity to consider why you teach, what qualities make effective teachers, and how you can develop those qualities.

Why Do We Teach?

Becoming a teacher is a vehicle for reaching the students we desire to guide, mentor, and teach. If we love our subject more than the students, we will fail. It is possible to last a whole career in the classroom teaching the same lessons year after year and never reach the soul of a student. In contrast, there are those who love to teach kids and let the learning take care of itself. These people want to interact with their students—to cry, laugh, and build relationships with them.

Building relationships is the foundation of quality instruction. Strauch (2004) found in her research that the engaged and stimulated student is less likely to be defiant. Experience teaches us that when students are actively involved and interested in what is being taught, their performance improves, class disruptions drop, and students begin to hold each other accountable. This is when teaching becomes enjoyable.

Qualities of Effective Teachers

Four qualities can be observed in effective teachers:

- **Desire**—The drive to work with young people and have a positive impact on their lives
- **Dedication**—The willingness to do whatever it takes to make an impact on students
- **Determination**—The energy to continue trying to reach students, regardless of whatever social or political issues get in the way
- **Discipline**—The self-discipline to set a positive and constructive example

Self-Assessment

In addition to assessing whether they have the four qualities mentioned above, teachers must consider whether they have attitudes that are conducive to effective classroom management. Managing the classroom is the first step leading to instructional success. A well-managed classroom invites teaching. Teaching leads to learning. Learning leads to application. Such things as disruptions, defiance, poor attitudes, lack of motivation, and outside influences interfere with instructional time. How the teacher responds to these interruptions determines the quantity and quality of instruction.

Several important questions can help you assess whether you are ready to construct and manage an effective classroom:

- Are you willing to invest time to build connections with all students?
- Can you accept the fact that there are times when the need for building relationships with students will supersede the need for instruction?
- Do you believe that acquiring knowledge about students will increase instructional time, and can you say how this will happen?
- What is your tolerance level for defiant behavior?
- Do you consistently address defiant behavior?

Similarly, it's worth evaluating your current interactions with students to determine how you might begin to increase your effectiveness:

- Do you look for a way to work with every student?
- Do you give up on students when their behavior seems too difficult to handle?
- Do you throw in the towel when the challenge is overwhelming?
- Do you lose control when you allow students to get you upset?

Remember This

Without the desire to find the good in every student, we will always fall short of our potential as teachers.

Remember This

Teachers are respected for their abilities to manage students, teach tough subjects, and maintain self-control. Be assured that you are appreciated and respected for doing what few others are able to accomplish or brave enough to pursue.

These are pivotal questions that must be addressed if you expect to have a working relationship with *each* student.

When our buttons get pushed and we are at the end of our patience, our patience always gives up before our will does. We can always dig a little deeper to meet the needs of our students, and ultimately ourselves. It's the individual who refuses to give up on a student who will have the greatest sense of accomplishment and satisfaction.

The tougher the student is to handle, the greater the opportunity for us to grow. If we are dedicated to the cause of seeing students gain our trust, then we will reap the reward of seeing them perform. Our task is to encourage the defiant students to perform for themselves. When students become self-starters, we can celebrate their success. Our efforts will not have been in vain. We will have accomplished what we set out to do—teach.

Student Assessment

In addition to self-assessment, student feedback is essential. Not only does it provide teachers with useful information about their teaching performance and the learning environments they have created, it also, in itself, empowers students. When students realize their input into the learning methodology and grading can be implemented into the operation of the classroom, they begin to develop a trusting relationship with the teacher. Learning improves, and disruptive and defiant behavior diminishes, due to student empowerment.

To increase the likelihood of getting honest, forthright feedback, teachers should provide students with an opportunity to provide an anonymous written evaluation, and students should be reminded not to put their names on the evaluations they turn in. Sample questions for an end-of-course evaluation might include these:

- What did you find most challenging about this course?
- What changes can you suggest about the course?
- What other topics or projects would you like to have studied?
- What was your favorite project or topic of study?
- What additional suggestions do you have?

Improving Your Skills

What's in Your Tool Box?

Throughout the course of a teaching career, educators will develop and acquire a variety of skills, methods, and strategies for teaching and working with students. As you continue to gain experience and knowledge, additional skills need to be added to the proverbial tool box. State and federal mandates also require the acquisition of additional skills.

A solid foundation for quality instruction can only be built with functional and appropriate tools. Knowing which tool or tools to apply in a given situation or setting requires an understanding of how the tool works. Most times this comes through trial and error, due to the uniqueness of each encounter with students. One of the goals of this book is to provide educators with additional tools that will help them make maximum use of instructional time. But they will need to practice with these new tools to determine when and how they can best use them.

How Sharp Are Your Tools?

Keeping our tools sharp is another necessity. As in any profession, if skills are not practiced and refined, we will not be at our best when

> **Remember This**
>
> We cannot save every child.
>
> There are students who have the intention to harm themselves. According to the National Council for Child Safety, youth suicide is a real and daily crisis. In these situations, rational thought has shut down, and a self-destruct mode has taken over. We might not be able to save these students, but we can make their lives a bit more pleasant while they are in our classrooms.
>
> Making sincere contact with such students creates a sense of openness and care. It is possible that the only kind words these students receive might very well be the ones they get from a caring teacher.

the moment of need arises. Sharpening takes place through open dialogue with colleagues, parents, and students. It's amazing what we can learn from talking to parents and students about our practices in the classroom. Openly acknowledging that we are not perfect will serve to keep us at the top of our profession.

Sharpening of our tools should take place on a regular basis. Attending in-service trainings and workshops as well as conferences designed around our particular disciplines is necessary for keeping up-to-date with changing issues and new developments. Staff development also provides encouragement for veteran teachers in the reinforcement of practices they have been using for years, and it opens doors to learning additional tips from other professional educators.

The reference to the professional educator is paramount. Professional educators will strive to improve their skills through continued dialogue with others, attendance at workshops and conferences, and work on innovative methods and strategies. These individuals rapidly gain the confidence of their colleagues and respect of their students. Learning in the environments they create becomes fun and stimulating.

The Need for New Tools

Veteran teachers are attending workshops for disruptive students as they sense the change in family culture and recognize the need to search out new approaches and interventions for working with defiant and disruptive students. Teachers who are well equipped to deal with curriculum and instruction must learn new tools for classroom management.

Training programs for aspiring young teachers must incorporate skills for working with disruptive and defiant students if these new teachers are to be kept in the field of education. Young teachers come into the field with great desire and passion. Veteran teachers can assist younger teachers through mentoring. Learning the art of teaching takes time and patience. Some will argue that teachers are born, not created. The truth is that nobody ever arrives at the immortalized state of grandmaster teacher.

The Bottom Line

Working with youngsters is a rewarding experience. Youngsters possess a natural energy and enthusiasm. When their energy is appreciated and drawn upon, adults can be reenergized. Adult experiences, coupled with youthful energy, bring about youthfulness in adults of all ages.

So is all this magic, or is it the natural response when students are provided with consistency and respect?

It isn't magic. When a student and teacher work together in an open and honest relationship, it's amazing how much more effective instructional time becomes. When students know their teacher truly cares, amazing student growth begins to take place.

I trust that you have found something useful in these pages. If you have questions, thoughts, or ideas, I can be reached at korbri@ gmail.com or pioneereducationconsulting.com.

References and Resources

Amenkhienan, C. (n.d.). *Attention deficit disorder student handbook.* Retrieved October 17, 2011, from http://www.ucc.vt.edu/stdysk/add3.html

Bandler, R., & Grinder, J. (1979). *Frogs into princes.* Moab, UT: Real People Press.

Bangert-Downs, R. L., Kulik, C. C., Kulik, J. A., & Morgan, M. (1991). The instructional effects of feedback in test-like events. *Review of Educational Research, 61*(2), 213–238.

Brookhart, S. M. (2008). *How to give effective feedback to your students.* Alexandria, VA: ASCD.

Brophy, J. (1996). *Teaching problem students.* New York, NY: Guilford Press.

Chandler, J. (n.d.). *Oppositional defiant disorder (ODD) and conduct disorder (CD) in children and adolescents: Diagnosis and treatment.* Retrieved October 17, 2011, from http://www.klis.com/chandler/pamphlet/oddcd/odd cdpamphlet.htm#_Toc121406203

Cheah, J. (2006). *Exploring how and why teenagers make decisions.* Retrieved from http://english.cmu.edu/inquiry/exploringdecisions.pdf

Covey, S. (1989). *The seven habits of highly effective people.* New York, NY: Simon & Schuster.

Cushman, K. (2003). *Respect, trust are part of the bargain for learning, teens say.* Retrieved from http://www.archachieve.net/smallschools/Resources/StudentVoice/firesarticle.pdf

Feinstein, S. G. (2004). *Secrets of the teenage brain: Research-based strategies for reaching and teaching today's adolescents.* Thousand Oaks, CA: Corwin.

Ford, D. Y., Alber, S. R., & Heward, W. L. (1998). Setting "motivation traps" for underachieving gifted students. *Gifted Child Today, 21*(2), 28–30, 32–33.

Gilbert, J. (2010). *Faculty voices: Giving timely student feedback.* Retrieved from http://web.byui.edu/LearningAndTeaching/post/2010/02/Faculty-Voices-Giving-Timely-Student-Feedback.aspx

Greer, T., & Farber, S. (n.d.). *Clinical teaching handbook.* Retrieved from http://www.fammed.washington.edu/network/FAV1–0000E799/CTHMain/Clinical%20Teaching%20Handbook.html

Grindeland, S. (2004, May 10). Student teacher: *The Seattle Times*. Retrieved from http://community.seattletimes.nwsource.com/archive/?date=200 40510&slug=grin11e

Gross Davis, B. (1993). *Tools for teaching*. San Francisco, CA: Jossey-Bass.

Hattie, J., & Timperley, H. (2007). The power of feedback. *Review of Educational Research, 77*(1), 81–112.

Hoffman Kaser, C. (2007). *Series on highly effective practices—Classroom expectations. 3. Establishing and teaching classroom expectations*. Retrieved from http://education.odu.edu/esse/research/series/expectations .shtml

Lehman, J. (2004). *The total transformation program*. Westbrook, ME: Legacy Publishing.

Lumsden, L. (1994). *Student motivation to learn*. Retrieved from http://eric .uoregon.edu/publications/digests/digest092.html

Maslow, A. H. (1943). *Motivation and personality*. New York, NY: Harper.

Meadows, R. J., & Blacher, J. H. (2002). *Difficult teens: A parent's guide for coping*. Ventura, CA: Meadow Oaks Press.

Middendorf, J., & Kalish, A. (1996). The "change-up" in lectures. *The National Teaching and Learning Forum, 5*(2). Retrieved from http://www.ntlf.com/ html/pi/9601/article1.htm

Payne, R. K. (2005). *A framework for understanding poverty* (4th rev. ed.). Highlands, TX: Aha Process.

Powell, S., & Nelson, B. (1997). Effects of choosing academic assignments on a student with attention deficit hyperactivity disorder. *Journal of Applied Behavioral Analysis, 30*(1), 181–183.

Rabiner, D. (2006). *Behavior disorders that often co-occur with ADHD*. Retrieved from http://www.helpforadd.com/co-occurring-disorders/

Raffini, J. (1993). *Winners without losers: Structures and strategies for increasing student motivation to learn*. Boston, MA: Allyn & Bacon.

Robb, M. (2001a). *Bringing up children*. Available from http://www.selfhelp guides.com/display.php3?guide=1885249587

Robb, M. (2001b). *Motivating students—Part 1*. Retrieved from http://www .suite101.com/article.cfm/social_emotional_learning/69938

Savannah Family Institute. [Producer]. (2006). *Understanding why your teen is out of control* (videotape). Parenting Your Out-of-Control Teenager Video Series. Available from http://www.difficult.net/video_info.asp#1

Seeman, H. (2006). *Preventing classroom discipline problems: A classroom management handbook*. Lanham, MD: Rowman & Littlefield.

Shimabukuro, S., Prater, M., Jenkins, A., & Edelen-Smith, P. (1999). The effects of self-monitoring of academic performance on students with learning disabilities and ADD/ADHA. *Education and Treatment of Children, 22*(4), 397–414.

Strauch, B. (2004). *The primal teen*. New York, NY: Anchor Books.

Sutton, J. D. (1997). Noncompliance: The "good kid" disorder. *Learning, 25*(4), 66–68.

Wees, D. (2010). *The role of immediacy of feedback in student learning*. Retrieved from http://davidwees.com/content/role-immediacy-feedback-student-learning

Wells, R. (2011). *Oppositional defiant (ODD) students: Must have methods.* Retrieved from http://addadhdadvances.com/ADHDparenting/103/oppositional-defiant-odd-students-must-have-methods/

Wooding, S. G. (2004). *Antidepressants and adolescents.* Retrieved from http://www.drwooding.com/archives/6

Woolsey-Terrazas, W., & Chavez, J. A. (2002). Strategies to work with students with oppositional defiant disorder. *Council for Exceptional Children TODAY, 8*(7). Retrieved from http://sesa.org/2002/04/strategies-to-work-with-students-with-oppositional-defiant-disorder/

Youth Change, Your Problem-Kid Problem Solver. (n.d.). http://www.youthchg.com

Ziglar, Z. (1985). *Raising positive kids in a negative world.* Nashville, TN: Oliver Nelson.

Index

NOTE: Illustrative material is identified by (fig.).

CORWIN

A SAGE Company

The Corwin logo—a raven striding across an open book—represents the union of courage and learning. Corwin is committed to improving education for all learners by publishing books and other professional development resources for those serving the field of PreK–12 education. By providing practical, hands-on materials, Corwin continues to carry out the promise of its motto: **"Helping Educators Do Their Work Better."**